OPENING THE DOORS

A PRISON CHAPLAIN'S LIFE ON THE INSIDE

PAUL GILL

WATERSIDE PRESS

Opening the Doors: A Prison Chaplain's Life on the Inside
Paul Gill

ISBN 978-1-909976-60-3 (Paperback)
ISBN 978-1-910979-61-7 (EPUB ebook)
ISBN 978-1-910979-62-4 (PDF ebook)

Cover Design by www.gibgob.com

All biblical quotations have been taken from *New Revised Standard Version Bible*, copyright © 1989 The Division of Christian Education of the National Council of the Churches of Christ in the United States of America. Used by permission. All rights reserved.

Printed by Lightning Source.

Main UK distributor Gardners Books, 1 Whittle Drive, Eastbourne, East Sussex, BN23 6QH. Tel: +44 (0)1323 521777; sales@gardners.com; www.gardners.com

North American distribution Ingram Book Company, One Ingram Blvd, La Vergne, TN 37086, USA. Tel: (+1) 615 793 5000; inquiry@ingramcontent.com

Cataloguing-In-Publication Data A catalogue record for this book can be obtained from the British Library.

e-book *Opening the Doors: A Prison Chaplain's Life on the Inside* is available as an ebook and also to subscribers of Ebrary, Ebsco, Myilibrary and Dawsonera.

Second Edition, Published 2018 by
Waterside Press Ltd
Sherfield Gables
Sherfield on Loddon, Hook
Hampshire RG27 0JG.

Telephone +44(0)1256 882250
Online catalogue WatersidePress.co.uk
Email enquiries@watersidepress.co.uk

Originally published in Australia in 2015 by Make Your Mark Publications.

AUTHOR'S NOTE

All stories within this book are compilations from many different scenarios in Australia, the UK, the USA and Europe. Most of the images were produced specifically for this publication. Models were used for the photos of prisoners, and all were electronically altered to disguise identities. Pseudonyms have been used throughout.

My commitment to authentically portraying the harshness of the prison environment included a decision to respect the cultural and social characteristics of prisoners' communications by not sanitising them. The book therefore contains coarse language which could be considered offensive in other contexts but is essential to understanding the desperation of those impacted by experiences of incarceration.

Remembering Rob

**A man of God,
friend, colleague,
chaplain extraordinaire**

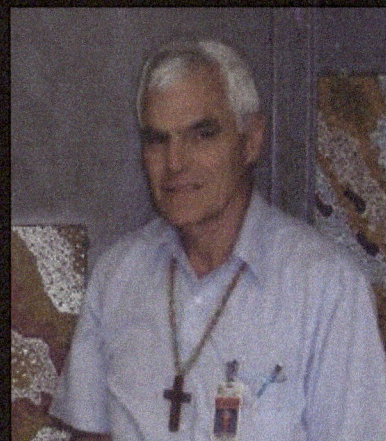

A WORD OF THANKS

First of all we give thanks to God who has given those of us involved in this project inspiration, and provided us with the wherewithal to complete the task. One of the things I have been conscious of from time to time, over the five years it has taken to complete the project, has been a sense of divine inspiration. In other words, the outcome is not been merely a result of human endeavour.

Thank you to the Reverend Dr Stephen Travis, formerly vice-principal of St John's College Nottingham, for the time and faith he has put into the project over several years.

Thank you to the congregation at St Philip's Cottesloe, Western Australia, especially Gary Davidson and John Pearman. The faithful prison ministry of people from this parish over many years has been, and continues to be, of enormous value in the work of the Kingdom of God amongst the most despised group of people in society. A particular thanks to those who have supported the production of this book: people have prayed, encouraged, and put their money where their faith is, thus enabling the project to be completed.

Thank you to Archbishop Roger Herft for his Foreword, and for his support for this project and for prison ministry throughout the Diocese of Perth.

Many thanks to the Australian Research Theology Foundation Inc., for providing finance to support the project.

Thanks also to the following people who have made a significant contribution to the publication of *Opening the Doors: A Chaplain's Life on the Inside* — the former Archbishop of Perth Dr Peter Carnley, who encouraged me to take up the role of prison chaplain; and Reverend Dr Charles Sherlock, whose incisive thinking helped me to sort out the wheat from the chaff from an enormous amount of material, and discard material that was 'interesting', but didn't quite fit.

Thank you to my wife Anne, without whose prayers, help and support this project would never have been completed — especially in regard to the application of her IT skills, which far exceed my own.

I would like to acknowledge the original publisher, Make Your Mark Publications (now known as 'Mono Unlimited') in Melbourne, Australia, and the work of Monique Lisbon and Fiona Dawn Hill in conceptualisation, editing, photography and book layout of the original publication.

Thank you to the men and women in prison, and some victims of crime, who trusted me enough to talk to me about the difficulties and challenges they faced in life: especially Mr Marcus Wellings who gave me permission to make use of his essay, 'The Invisible Man'. Marcus was executed by the State of Georgia, USA, on 17 June 2014, after spending 22 years on death row.

It is my hope and prayer that this book, along with other initiatives, will play a small part in reducing the number of people who are sent to prison and, in so doing, reduce the number of victims of crime.

Paul Gill
August 2018

FOREWORD

Imprisonment, slavery, oppression and captivity form an essential part of the story of faith. Places of darkness and despair provide the context for the cataclysmic saving acts of God. Most of the letters of the New Testament are forged in the midst of chains.

Prisons play a paradoxical role. They are punitive. The system seeks to teach offenders a lesson, to keep communities safe and to recognise the harm perpetrated on the victims of crime. They are restorative — in the midst of brutality and violence they hope to rehabilitate offenders.

The system has a pervasive way of controlling those given responsibility to transform lives in their care. No-one escapes the cycles of violence as human dignity is sacrificed on the vote-catching mantra of law and order. An ignorant media proclaims the catchphrase: 'Lock them up and throw away the key'.

Incarceration can become the wilderness in which cycles of despair gain momentum.

Paul Gill has lived and ministered in 'corrective services'. The ministry has left its scars. The role of the chaplain is that of priest, pastor and prophet to all in the system — the victims of crime, the perpetrators, the officials in the gaol, policy makers, families and the community at large.

Paul describes the environment as he finds it. He refuses to gloss over the dysfunctionality in home and family, in society at large, that shapes the thinking, feeling and behaviour of those who end up in the prison system. He is angered at the opposition to programmes based on the precepts of restorative justice. Paul agonises over those who are in need of mental health care.

Paul sits with those who live in exile. He dares to hope for a day when the cycle of violence will be broken. Through art, poetry, literature and seeing every person as made in God's image, Paul offers an alternate reality in which sinner and sinned against may touch each other's wounds, making costly mutual healing a possibility.

Opening the Doors speaks to all of us. Whether we admit it or not, we inhabit a world in which bars and walls contain us. Those who are captive in the system can cry out:

> Stone walls do not a prison make,
> nor iron bars a cage;
> minds innocent and quiet take
> that for a hermitage.
> If I have freedom in my love,
> and in my soul am free,
> angels alone, that soar above,
> enjoy such liberty.[1]

The power of God in Christ helps us all, angels and demons, to recognise our imprisonment. The love of God in cross and resurrection gifts us with the glorious liberty of being the children of God.

The Most Reverend Roger Herft AM
Former Anglican Archbishop of Perth and Metropolitan of the Province of Western Australia

---

1   Richard Lovelace, *To Althea, from Prison*, 1649.

CONTENTS

Opening the Doors

INTRODUCTION
GOD BEHIND BARS

THE **SPIRIT** OF THE SOVEREIGN LORD IS ON ME, BECAUSE THE **LORD** HAS ANOINTED ME TO PREACH GOOD NEWS TO THE POOR. HE HAS **SENT** ME TO BIND UP THE BROKEN HEARTED, TO PROCLAIM FREEDOM FOR THE CAPTIVES AND RELEASE FROM DARKNESS FOR THE PRISONERS. ISAIAH 61:1

Working as a Prison Chaplain is a challenging but fulfilling vocation to which some are called. Every day I felt I was doing something that was worthwhile and mattered to the people I was working with. The main requirement is to be a person of integrity who has got a firm historical and objective foundation for their faith. St Paul, writing to the Corinthians, said: 'If Christ has not been raised [from the dead] then our proclamation has been in vain, and your faith has been in vain'. (I Corinthians Chapter 15) The idea of things seeming to be 'in vain' is very common to people behind bars who are often lost, disorientated, and uncertain of everything. Questions they have, often unspoken, are: 'Who am I?' 'Have I any future?' 'Is it worth living another day?' 'Does anyone care about me?'

Chaplains need to be clear about their role in the prison community, and it is a community of sorts. They are not social workers, psychologists, educators, mental health workers or medics. They work alongside all of these people but their main concern is the spiritual dimension of life, getting alongside people and sharing the love and grace of God which translates into building genuine relationships with what are sometimes the most unlikely people.

Many prisoners have little experience of positive relationships with genuine trustworthy warm hearted people, that is, the experience of love. On the contrary their role models have often exhibited violence, thieving and addiction as being 'normal', so they have grown up with a sense that their survival is dependent on these 'norms'. Someone highlighting the importance of human beings experiencing love wrote: 'The power of love is not an optional extra, but one of the constitutive elements that is as necessary to the human person as, oxygen, food, and water'.[1]

There are always exceptions to the above. For example, the 18-year-old university student on a night out with his girlfriend. He has had too much to drink and overreacts when he punches a guy who he thinks has said something insulting about his lady friend. The guy falls over and hits his head on the concrete floor. Three days later he dies in hospital as a result of head trauma. His assailant is arrested, locked-up and charged with manslaughter. Incidents such as this happen all too frequently and have a devastating effect on family and friends of the victim, and the assailant.

A Christian prison officer said to me one day words to the effect that she could: 'feel the power of evil' in the prison in which we both worked. She was rather taken aback when I responded by saying that: 'I feel the power of God'—in our workplace. In other words, wherever there are people suffering, where their lives are dysfunctional and disintegrating, God is to be found. Jesus caused consternation on one occasion when he identified Himself with people in prison. He said, when you visit them you are visiting me, when you look into their faces, you will see my face. (Matthew 25: 36–45). All of us bear the scars of living, none of us are perfect. Behind every face there is a human being for whom Christ died. The work of the pastor, priest, minister, padre and chaplain is to encourage by example and word the realisation of this, so that people's lives are renewed and changed. It is never too late for this to happen.

---

1   Paul Tillich, *Love, Power and Justice*, Abingdon Press, 26.

The chapel at Wormwood Scrubs Prison UK

CHAPTER 1

ON THE INSIDE

·3·6m·

·2·8m·

Where the Money Is

A judge who was about to sentence a man who had been convicted of attempted bank robbery for the umpteenth time, asked: 'Why do you keep trying to rob banks?' After a long pause, the man in the dock said: 'Because that's where the money is!'

Beginning a new job in a maximum security prison is never easy. It is an atypical environment that can be dangerous. So, I arrived for my first day with some trepidation.

In the minds of other staff there would have been questions such as: Will this newcomer put us at risk by his lack of awareness of the pitfalls and dangers? Is the new chaplain a 'Bible basher' who strives to see people 'converted' and changed overnight? Is he going to be easy to manipulate? Will he be taken in by the sob stories of prisoners who are masters of deception?

Starting Work

It takes at least a year to begin to establish credibility with prison staff as a trustworthy and balanced chaplain who can function appropriately in prisons. In every prison there will be a minority of staff who see chaplains as nothing more than 'dodgy do-gooders'. Other staff will have a more balanced awareness and some experience of the spiritual dimension of life. They know from experience that chaplaincy can bring about change in the lives of the most unlikely people. Some staff take a pragmatic view. They know that difficult prisoners sometimes calm down when they have spoken with a chaplain about issues that are causing them distress. Peaceful outcomes are good for everyone.

New chaplains are shown around and undergo an orientation process which outlines the 'do's and don'ts' within the institution. They are issued with photo identification tags that must be clearly visible at all times within the prison, including entry and exit points. Then they are issued with keys that must be handed in when leaving. It is the unforgivable sin for those who work in prisons to lose their keys. Such negligence compromises security and safety. Replacing or recalibrating most of the locks and keys on-site would be expensive, time-consuming and have a negative effect on staff and prisoners. I quickly obtained a key pouch so my keys were not visible. It was rumoured that some clever inmates could replicate keys just by seeing them. I also obtained a chain and attached one end securely to my belt and the other to my keys, before going into any area where there were prisoners. The chain was long enough for me to lock and unlock gates and doors without ever having to unhook my keys.

It can be very disconcerting to be under security camera surveillance most of the time. However, this is a necessary safety feature which enables security staff to locate anyone, at any time, via monitors. I gradually got to know my way around and started to get to know everyone.

It is challenging working out how to approach, support and relate to people who have committed the most appalling crimes, including serial killers, paedophiles, drug traffickers, sexual offenders and murderers. Overall, I found that it is best not to know about the crimes that people have committed, although, as these details are often plastered all over the media, it becomes impossible to block this out entirely.

The longer I worked in prisons, the more I came to know about the people living within those walled communities. When prisoners began to trust me, they sometimes wanted to talk about their offending behaviour. I would hear about prisoners' backgrounds during various staff meetings. Some prisoners would talk to me about others, saying: 'I am not as bad as him. I have done armed robberies but he has murdered someone.' I nearly always found that people in prison bore little resemblance to how they had been portrayed in the media. Invariably media reports exaggerate aspects of cases that involve issues of violence or sex.

As I went about my days within the prisons, I found that I did not actually spend much time thinking about the crimes that had been committed. After all, I was not part of the justice system that had apprehended, tried, convicted and imprisoned these people. My role was to give support, solace and advice if I was asked to do so.

Prisoners — Who Are They?

The population of the prisons in most western countries is disproportionately made up of those at the lower end of the socio-economic scale, including: those struggling with mental health issues; the unemployed; the homeless; indigenous people; and other minority groups facing discrimination. Most children and juveniles in prison come mainly from backgrounds of neglect and abuse. In the industrialised world, many countries have increased their prison populations over the last three decades to include people living with mental illness, those suffering from addiction, and others experiencing social exclusion.

I certainly didn't find too many bankers, doctors, university professors, farmers and shop-keepers in prison!

Prisoners are people, a fact that is easily forgotten. For various reasons they have behaved in ways that are unacceptable in mainstream society, so they have been incarcerated. In theory, in western democracies, the purpose of imprisonment is to provide opportunities for rehabilitation so offenders can return to society and make positive contributions. However, this does not happen often enough.

People do not just wake up one morning and think to themselves: 'I am going to commit an armed robbery today,' or 'I am going to assault or kill someone today.' There is always background and context.

Why are people sent to prison? People end up in prison for different, but often interrelated, reasons.

Crimes of Passion

There is a significant number of 'one-crime' prisoners who end up in gaol simply because a wave of emotion pushes them over the edge and they impulsively commit a very serious offence. Such 'crimes of passion' are almost always prompted by high levels of psychological stress, sometimes deliberate blackmail, usually about access or lack of access to children. Ninety-eight percent of such perpetrators could go back into mainstream society and never commit another criminal act. Given a fair chance, they could live as ordinary upright citizens for the rest of their lives. So, in a sense, it is a waste of time and money to keep them in prison. However, such offenders have to learn (the hard way) that they cannot escape the consequences of violent behaviour. Also, victims, their families and communities need a sense of justice for healing to begin. Perpetrators cannot be allowed to just walk away.

Mental Health Issues

Mental illness is a significant factor in the lives of many people who are imprisoned. I feel particular compassion for those affected because of my own experiences of chronic depression throughout most of my adult life. I have had to learn to manage this illness with the assistance of cognitive behavioural therapy and medication. So I can say with certainty, prison is the worst possible place for people living with mental health issues.

Many prisoners are suffering from serious mental illnesses when they enter prison. A significant number leave prison in a worse state than on arrival. A senior medical person who runs a small, secure mental health facility once commented: 'What these people need is hospital treatment, and that's what they get when they are here, not punishment. Facilities like these need to be vastly and urgently expanded. Our patients need treatment. Many of them would get better and learn to manage their illnesses so they could live most of their lives in mainstream society.'

When I walked into this particular facility, the atmosphere was quite different from prison, where there was tension, a brooding fear and the potential for violence to break out at any moment. In this facility, people are treated as individuals, rather than part of a large mass where their individual identity is lost. Patients are allowed to wear their own clothes and are addressed by their first name. These basic courtesies enable them to maintain or begin to establish dignity. Such mixed gender facilities also encourage civility and peer support. Instead of everything being painted in a depressing off-white colour, the environment is conducive to lifting patients' spirits. Rooms are decorated in bright colours. There are pictures on the walls, and furniture in the open areas is varied. Staff are dressed in civilian clothes rather than pseudo-military uniforms. Some patients begin to find a sense of hope. They realise that perhaps life can be more than just a daily battle to survive on the margins of society.

An inpatient named Colin said: 'I feel better in here. I am not constantly afraid. I don't need to watch my back all the time. We talk in a group. Some people talk about their lives. I am not the only one who has fucked up. I hope I can stay here for a bit, but because it's so small I expect it won't be long. The hospital chaplain came round and talked to me. It was good. He made me think.'

Of course, in such facilities, there are still rules and regulations. The place has to be tightly controlled to keep everyone safe and to ensure that patients get the most benefit from their stay. However, this is achieved in a firm but gentle way rather than through oppressive bullying. This makes a huge difference.

Large, secure, well-built and adequately resourced mental health facilities would improve the quality of life for people who are living with serious mental illnesses and who land in the prison system. Prisons have neither the mandate nor the expertise to cope with the complexities of mental health issues. Economically, in the longer run, such a strategy would significantly reduce the number of mandatory admissions, saving governments huge amounts of money. Socially, there would be less crime and fewer victims. Society would benefit in every way.

Career Criminals

Most career criminals make a conscious choice to pursue activities outside the law for economic gain. I note that such offenders accept that a proportion of their lives will inevitably be spent in prison. However, they decide that the rewards outweigh this inconvenience. Career criminals tend to be people of above average intelligence. They are articulate 'wheelers and dealers'. They often become involved in crime by dealing in large amounts of contraband, laundering money and through tax evasion. Usually career criminals are part of a wide network that extends throughout the country and internationally. They tend not to work alone but are part of bigger organisations. They typically lead lavish lifestyles, fly first class, drive expensive vehicles, enjoy extravagant holidays and spend large amounts of money without a second thought. One guy described the expensive and prolonged holidays that he and his associates had in Thailand. 'There were always plenty of hookers, drugs and booze,' he said. 'We spent most days around the pool and most nights partying.'

Career criminals are not easy to catch because they have sophisticated defence mechanisms, both electronic and otherwise. Similarly, it is difficult to bring them to conviction, because their organisations spend large sums of money to 'slush-fund' their legal representation. If they happen to be convicted, expensive lawyers continue to trawl through trial manuscripts looking for points of law as grounds for appeal. When career criminals do serve time in prison, their organisations expect them to 'keep their head down' and not reveal anything about their network and its activities. Representatives of crime organisations visit prisons to reassure their apprehended associates that they are not forgotten and to remind them of responsibilities to keep quiet. Some have a bit of a Robin Hood worldview and can be quite generous in looking after people, both in prison and on the outside. Other prisoners tend to be wary of career criminals because of their reputations and associates.

Career criminal prisoners usually have well thought-out moral and ethical frameworks of their own. For example, some will traffic large amounts of cocaine but not heroin. One guy explained it like this: 'Cocaine should be decriminalised. For most people, it's a harmless recreational drug and not really addictive. I don't think I am doing anyone any harm trafficking it.' He conveniently forgot the murder and mayhem that takes place in countries like Honduras, where rival gangs battle to control the importation of cocaine into the USA. He continued: 'Heroin is different, highly addictive and destroys people's lives. I would never be involved in bringing it into the country and spreading it around.'

Career criminals also tend to avoid violence, or at least keep it at arm's length. Pragmatically, it draws attention to the organisation and its activities. To them, violence is inconvenient, repugnant and usually unnecessary.

Some of these people appear to have a genuine appreciation of the spiritual dimension of life. They talk about their 'faith' quite openly, attend chapel services and Bible studies and see no contradiction between faith and their chosen profession.

Falsely Convicted?

When I tell people about my work in prisons, they often respond: 'And, I bet the prisoners all claim to be innocent!' While some falsely claim to be innocent, there are others who have been wrongly convicted.

For about a year, I had conversations with a man on remand who was accused of multiple offences. He frequently claimed to be innocent and I got to the point of almost believing him. When he gave evidence at his trial, I was in the public gallery. He was cross-examined by the prosecuting counsel and it soon became clear to everyone in court, including the jury, that he was guilty. He subsequently received a substantial term of imprisonment.

Another man asked to see me and told me his version of his arrest for involvement in an armed robbery. He said:

> I was sitting in my car with the engine running looking at a map because I was lost. Suddenly, this geezer with a balaclava on his head rushed out of the bank. I didn't know I was parked in front of the bank. He jumped in my car, shoved a shot-gun in my face and said, 'Drive!' So I did. We had only gone two blocks when we were surrounded by armed police at a road-block and arrested. I tried to explain but they didn't believe me. Now I'm on remand waiting trial for armed robbery. It's not fair.

The only response I could give was: 'Talk to your lawyer.' However, it transpired that no-one, including the jury, believed his version of events. He was convicted and received a substantial term of imprisonment.

Most claims of false conviction peter out as time goes on. The crunch comes when a bid to maintain innocence risks a prisoner being disadvantaged as a result of their denial. Such behaviour might risk parole dates being pushed back. Some prisoners continue to maintain claims of innocence throughout their sentences. Freddie had been in prison for more than 30 years. He told me he had been sentenced to death as a result of being wrongfully convicted of killing a police officer. His sentence was later commuted to life in prison. When he was old and sick, he could have been released had he admitted his guilt. However, he maintained his innocence until the grave.

It sometimes becomes evident that some people have been falsely convicted when their convictions are overturned on appeal. It is now possible to gather DNA from evidential exhibits related to cases in which the convicted person may have been in prison for many years. In the light of new evidence, sometimes people are proved innocent. It is, of course, too late for those who have been convicted of capital crimes and executed. So, sadly, there were 358 post-conviction DNA exonerations in the USA up to July 2018.[1] One can only speculate as to how many people have been executed who should have been exonerated.

Such miscarriages of justice occur because, like every other human organisation, the justice system is fallible and, from time to time, corrupt. Sometimes officials tell lies. Evidence can be withheld or manipulated. When a particularly heinous crime has been committed, investigators are put under enormous pressure to apprehend the offender. Sometimes vulnerable people are scapegoated as investigators yield to the temptation to pin the offence on 'someone … anyone will do!'

Such was the case with Joey. He was very vulnerable around the time when someone was murdered in his neighbourhood. He was picked up by the police, charged with murder, convicted and given a life sentence. After numerous appeals and community support from a wide variety of people, Joey was exonerated. He had served seven years of a life sentence.

It is impossible to give reliable statistics about the rates of false imprisonment. Some cases will never be known, but there is no doubt that a few innocent people are convicted and imprisoned. Those who suffer this fate are robbed of life, time, relationships and opportunities. That which is lost can never be regained, and it hurts.

---

1   See www.innocenceproject.org, accessed July 2018.

One person in prison used the following poem to express, as he saw it, the reason for his messed-up life:

THEY FUCK YOU UP YOUR MUM AND DAD.
THEY MAY NOT MEAN TO BUT THEY DO.
THEY FILL YOU WITH THE FAULTS THEY HAD
AND ADD SOME EXTRA JUST FOR YOU.

BUT THEY WERE FUCKED UP IN THEIR TURN
BY FOOLS IN OLD-STYLE HATS AND COATS,
WHO HALF THE TIME WERE SOPPY-STERN
AND HALF AT ONE ANOTHER'S THROATS.

MAN HANDS ON MISERY TO MAN.
IT DEEPENS LIKE A COASTAL SHELF.
GET OUT AS EARLY AS YOU CAN,
AND DON'T HAVE ANY KIDS YOURSELF.

Philip Larkin, 'This Be The Verse'.[1]

---

1   Used by permission of the Society of Authors as the literary representative of the estate of Philip Larkin. Source: *Collected Poems* (New York: Farrar Straus and Giroux, 2001).

I Couldn't Help It

Joe had been brought up in the middle of crime and violence, mainly perpetrated by his father as he was growing up. He said: 'Dad was a chronic alcoholic, violent towards mum and anyone else, including kids, if they got in his way. From a very early age, I was in the way. That bastard used to knock us about.' His perception was that to survive, stealing and violence were essential. One of the most disturbing things I ever heard was Joe's statement: 'The main thing I learned, as I grew up, was that there is no-one I can trust.' Joe learnt from his family and wider environment that thieving and violence were 'normal' and essential to survival.

So, as a child, Joe was always on the alert and ready to react aggressively in any situation. Unfortunately, he carried this with him into adult life. He was a big guy. He said: 'When I hit someone, they usually go down and stay down. If they are getting up I put the boot in.' On one occasion, when he was on the outside, he was in a bar having a drink with his 'lady friend' when someone accidentally brushed past, causing some of his beer to slop out of his glass onto his shoes. His reaction was completely out of proportion. He turned and smashed his glass over the head of the person who had offended him. The victim was stitched up in hospital. Joe was sent back to prison. There, he commented: 'I thought this bloke was having a go at me and I had to "do" him before he "did" me. I couldn't help it — that's how I am.'

I pointed out to Joe that people can change and that there was hope for him to change as well. I also reminded him that, while he was in prison, there would be opportunities to participate in courses such as anger management and cognitive behavioural skills. These programmes could help him build up the skills necessary to cope with stressful situations on the outside so that he would not keep returning to prison. I also invited Joe to think about the spiritual dimension of life by attending one of the courses we ran in the chapel. Here, he would hear stories of people from similar backgrounds who had changed as a result of finding faith.

Over the years, I did not see any great change in Joe. But, moving around the prison, I would see him fairly frequently and he was always happy to stop and have a chat. Many prison inmates mellow as they get older. I always hoped and prayed that Joe might be one of them.

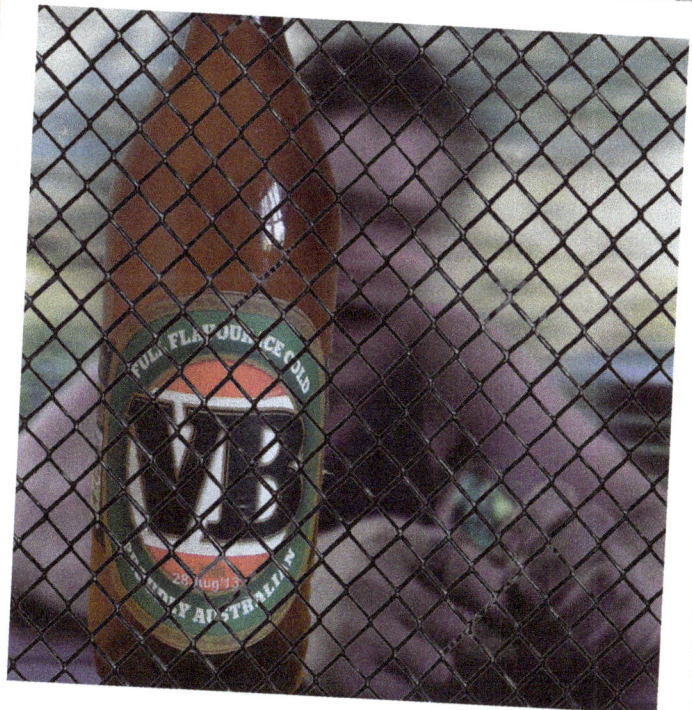

We Are All Potential Prisoners

I discovered that most people within the prisons know that chaplains represent God, faith, repentance and forgiveness, but are not necessarily able to articulate that. I held tight to my belief that Christ had died for them, just as He had for me. That became the basis of our conversations and I was very interested to see where that would lead us.

According to the letter of the law, every one of us is a potential prisoner. Most of us have 'trespassed' in spite of a sign that says 'No Trespassing'. No driver has ever totally abided by the law. I recently got a ticket for speeding. Ideally, the law is meant to be applied with a degree of flexibility and compassion. Not everything is black or white. If everyone who broke the law were to be imprisoned, we would all be in prison! (There is, of course, a huge difference between driving too fast and committing an armed robbery!)

However, the fact stands that no-one can be perfect all of the time.

Letter from a Traumatised Family

Lord God,
I received this letter
…from the family of a murder victim.
Joanne was only 19 when she was killed.
The bloke who killed her
has been here about a year.
I saw him yesterday.

The family tells me
that they are as heartbroken now
as they were when the police first told them
…of Joanne's death.

Lord, they feel
as if they have been left in the dark.
Why did it happen?
What led to it?
Why did Jimmy do what he did?
Has he expressed any remorse?
What does a 'life' sentence mean?
How long or short will it be?

In the dark
…because Jimmy pleaded guilty.
There was no trial.
No public accountability.
The police helped as much as they could
…but Lord, it wasn't enough!

Lord,
They have written to me,
…because they want to meet Jimmy!
They want conversation.
They think it might help.
They don't seem angry
…only sad and bewildered.

Oh God!
The problem is…
Jimmy is also sad and bewildered.
Perhaps, if they were sad and bewildered
    …together
      …it just might help them all.

But Lord,
when I asked Jimmy,
he said, 'No.'
He is unwell,
emotionally and psychologically.
I think he might come round to it,
eventually,
but, not now.

I have arranged to go and see the family
this afternoon.
I don't know if they believe in you, Lord,
But I am going in your name.

I'd like to bring them
comfort and support.
I feel very inadequate
and a little nervous.
Please lead the way.

I am going to continue seeing Jimmy
here in the years to come.
He's only 21 and in desperate
need of comfort and support.

A moment of madness
destroyed Joanne's life;
his life;
the lives of many;
their whole families.

But Lord,
help me to put first things first.
Be with me today
as I go to visit Joanne's family.

Fighting Ever Since[1]

I was asked to visit Johnny, a prisoner in his 50s who had spent most of his adult life in prison, mainly as a result of assaults and fighting.

After a few very general conversations which enabled us to get to know each other, he began talking about his life. He had been brought up in a deprived area of Melbourne.

At the age of 12, he and some friends threw stones at shop windows and broke them. Following this incident and several others, he was rejected by his parents and placed in a residential home for disturbed children.

During his first month there, he was badly beaten by a group of 17 year olds. Several times he tried to run away but he was always caught, brought back and caned by the head of the institution.

He told one of the other kids that he had decided to commit suicide but didn't know how to do it.

The other kid said: 'Don't kill yourself; learn to fight.'

'But I'm too small to fight,' said Johnny.

'Then, I'll teach you to fight!' said the other kid.

Johnny said to me: 'He did teach me to fight, and I've been fighting ever since!'

It had never occurred to Johnny that it is possible to live without physical violence, because it had always been present in his life. It was all he had ever known.

People's backgrounds are very varied. For some, experiences in early life lead them into trouble, including time in prison.

---

1   Adapted from Patrick Hannon, 'Law and Morality' in *Justice Reflections* 1, J5, www.justicereflections.org.uk, accessed August 2013.

In a Bad State

For years, Josh suffered from major depression. He usually managed to live satisfactorily with the help of medication and cognitive behavioural therapy. However, from time to time, things started to run out of control and he needed a few days in hospital. The story of his incarceration is a combination of tragic circumstances and events:

I had been feeling unwell for a few days but my GP refused to give me a referral for assessment at the psychiatric ward of my local hospital. He suggested I persevere for a few more days to see if I could get back on track. On the Friday evening, I was getting worse and had thoughts of suicide. I rang the hospital and asked if they would see me but they refused unless I had a referral. By Saturday evening, I was desperate and rang the hospital again. They could tell I was in a bad state and agreed to see me. Having no immediate family or friends close by, and little money, I decided to drive to the hospital even though I knew I wasn't really in a fit state to do so. On the way to the hospital, I had a serious accident and hit an elderly man who was badly injured and died the next day. The police came. I was arrested for dangerous driving and held in a cell overnight. The charges against me were upgraded and, on the Monday morning, I was remanded in custody.

Josh was eventually convicted of causing death by dangerous driving and received a lengthy prison sentence.

Josh's account of what happened resonated with me. I had the good fortune to be able to get medical help when I needed it. I recall on one occasion, I was driving with excessive adrenalin due to the effects of my depression. Fortunately, I was able to get home safely and my wife was there to take me to hospital.

A Moment of Madness

Michael came across as an educated, articulate man. He described the events leading to his incarceration as follows:

Sometimes I think of being in prison and the events that led to it as a nightmare that I am going to wake up from. My family and I had just about everything we wanted, a lovely home in a smart suburb near the beach. We had three children, two girls and a boy, happy kids doing well at school and enjoying life.

I was working for an oil company and earning big bucks. I had to travel overseas three or four times a year for several weeks, often at short notice. My wife started to complain about me 'being away all the time', which was a bit of an exaggeration really. She enjoyed the lifestyle but didn't like me being away, which was understandable, I guess. It got to the point where she said: 'One of these days I won't be here when you get back.' I didn't take this seriously until it happened.

On my return home from one trip, she and the kids were gone. She had left a letter saying she wanted a divorce and included the name of her solicitor who I should contact. I was devastated. I didn't know where they were. I was desperate to see her and the kids but her solicitor wouldn't tell me where they were. To cut a long story short, I eventually found them and reluctantly agreed to a separation and to work towards joint custody of the children. They would live with her because I had to go away on business for indeterminate lengths of time several times a year, but I would have full access to them when I was at home. Gradually I saw less and less of the children. When I was home there always seemed to be an excuse why they couldn't be with me.

I got frustrated and angrier and angrier. I started drinking too much. I couldn't concentrate on my work and things were spiraling out of control. One evening, I went to their house. I knew the kids were away at their grandparents' and my intention was to talk to Janet and see if we could sort things out. When I got there she didn't seem really interested in talking about things, so we ended up having a heated argument. I lost it, picked something up and hit her over the head and kept hitting her. She died the next day in hospital.

Michael is now serving a life sentence for murder with a minimum tariff of 14 years. A moment of madness irrevocably changed his life, devastatingly impacting his family, He said: 'I am a murderer. My kids are with their grandparents. I don't deserve to live. My life is over.'

Michael was in a very dark place. He needed a reason to go on living—a sense of hope for the future.

I assured Michael of this hope. He was a relatively young man who had committed a serious crime. On the other hand, he had admitted guilt, accepted responsibility, and was suffering consequences.

I reminded him that he would only be in his 40s when he got out. He would still have a lot of living to do. In the meantime, there were various educational and recreational opportunities on offer. Sometimes people in prison discover talents that they previously did not know they possessed. There are also worthwhile and responsible jobs within prisons for people who are cooperative, capable and trustworthy.

Initially, Michael was uncertain about talking with me. He had assumed our conversations would be primarily about religion. Then, I said something that surprised him. I am a person of faith but not particularly religious in the sense that the trappings of religion have never assumed great importance for me. I believe in faith, prayer and the presence of God. I also have conviction that, however bleak things may seem, there is always hope. Hope always overcomes despair, just as light shines in the darkness and darkness can never put it out (John 1:5). It is my hope that our conversations helped Michael to begin the task of rebuilding his life.

A Man of Faith

Paul is a man of faith who always attended chapel services, Bible studies and other activities that I organised. His faith is a big factor in enabling him to maintain his dignity and not succumb to hopelessness, despair, bitterness and anger. I continue to feel personally disturbed about Paul's conviction. I believe that his alleged victim was under the influence of someone who was antagonistic towards him. It would not have taken much to manipulate this woman to give false evidence. An added complication was that Paul's conviction opened the way for the alleged victim to receive monetary compensation and the third person also benefitted economically. Such scenarios cause alarm bells to ring for me, particularly when there is a profit to be made by a 'victim' and their 'hangers on' as the result of a conviction.

Hope

People in prison are not all the same, and are imprisoned for all sorts of different reasons. A criminal act does not take place in isolation from the perpetrator's social, cultural and historical contexts. There are often patterns of vulnerability that diminish people's chances of living productively in mainstream society without getting tangled up in crime.

In general terms, there are five factors that set people on a path toward prison. The first is lack of education (about 60 percent of adult male prisoners have a reading age of eight years or less). Next is lack of job skills (about 80 percent are unemployed at the time of their arrest). Third is lack of social skills (many have never learned basic skills required to live in society, such as taking responsibility, parenting, respecting other people and their property and even punctuality, to equip them to hold down a job). Next is undiagnosed and untreated mental illness and, finally, substance abuse. (More than 70 percent of people received into prison are, or have been, affected by alcohol and other drug misuse.)

In the end, we all have to take responsibility for our own lives and what we do with them. However, the hand of cards we are dealt in life, particularly our upbringing, is bound to have a significant effect. There are always exceptions to this general rule — those with the best of everything can still end up in prison and those with the worst possible beginning can develop into stable, law-abiding citizens.

If a person does end up in prison, what happens during incarceration will largely determine what route they will take once they are released. In some jurisdictions, society shoots itself in the foot by imposing a negative and brutal regime on prisoners so that, when they are released, they are even less able to live peacefully and productively in mainstream society than when they were first admitted. One prisoner said, the day before his release: 'I've had a tough time in here. Once I'm out, I will get my revenge on those who grassed me up.' I pointed out that his desire for revenge would probably result in him returning to prison before too long. His response was: 'I don't give a fuck. I have to get my revenge.'

On the other hand, there is always a possibility that prisoners will be rehabilitated and able to return to mainstream society. I believe rehabilitation is most likely to occur when the prison regime is firm, fair, and enables people to maintain or discover dignity through participating in activities such as education, social skills learning programmes, counselling for drug and alcohol addictions, anger management, and cognitive behavioural therapy.

From a Christian perspective and, arguably that of most other religious traditions, there is always hope in the providence of God. No-one is beyond receiving the gift of grace and its possibilities for transformation.

CHAPTER 2

IN THE NICK

Untouched Morning Tea

A careers officer went into a prison with two trainees to assist soon-to-be released prisoners with issues associated with their future employment. They were shown into a room where a trusted prisoner was preparing morning tea for them. One of the trainees asked the supervising prison officer: 'Why is this guy in prison?' The reply was: 'He murdered someone by poisoning them.' Years later, telling this story the former careers officer said: 'Morning tea remained untouched.'

Newcomers

When a person enters prison, an initial assessment is made on arrival to see if they are at risk. The trauma of arrest and imprisonment can be so great that people are often placed initially into a Special Care Unit (SCU) where they can be observed 24/7 to keep them safe from others and sometimes from themselves.

Some people are so terrified at coming into prison that it is advisable not to place them into the mainstream (sometimes called normal location) immediately. Their obvious fear makes them vulnerable to sexual and other violent predators. Prison chaplains try to see all newcomers, unless individuals decline to see them.

The 'Big House'

When I visited James the morning after his admission, he was cowering in his cell, very frightened and in tears. He told me that it was his 18th birthday and that he had been transferred from a juvenile facility to the adult prison. James would remember his 18th birthday for all the wrong reasons! He was quite a big lad and had no problem looking after himself in the juvenile system. However, the place where he was now, known by some as the 'Big House', was a very different proposition. James realised that his place in the pecking order had gone from top to bottom. He was terrified: 'I can't do this. I've heard about this place. People get bashed up and raped.'

I gave him reassurance that, as it was his first time in an adult prison, he would be placed in a unit where he would be at minimum risk. The staff would look after him, as would the peer support prisoners. (Sometimes it is possible to organise a tough prisoner, with a reputation, who has turned over a new leaf, to take a vulnerable prisoner under his wing. The word gets round to potential predators, 'this guy is being looked after ... don't mess with him.')

James was eventually transferred to a mainstream unit and acclimatised with no more than the usual problems for a young first-timer.

'Old Lags'

At the other end of the spectrum are 'old lags' like Billy.

Billy was an alcoholic in his 50s who had been in and out of prison for years. His offences were relatively minor and he had never been violent. When he was in prison he was always compliant with the regime. One day, the police spotted him on the street and knew that there was a warrant out for his arrest, so he was arrested. There was a minor scuffle and Billy's glasses were broken.

When he arrived at the prison he was upset and agitated but not violent. He was temporarily placed in a safe cell under observation. He said: 'They roughed me up. They didn't need to. You know I am not a violent person. I would have come quietly. My glasses got broken. I can't see without them.'

As I listened to his story, he calmed down. After a while, I went to get him some replacement spectacles.

No Prior Warning

Some people brought into prison by the police have been snatched off the street. Others are arrested in their homes with no prior warning. For some, this means they lose just about everything. Jack was arrested in his council flat. He lived alone and had no relatives. It had taken years for him to reach the top of the housing waiting list.

While he was on remand, he worried:

If I don't pay my rent, I will lose my home. The security is not good. The place will be wrecked. All my things will either be stolen or sold off and I will be back on the street. If that happens, I won't survive. I am too old to go back to that.

As it turned out, on that occasion, he was released later that day without charge. His home was still intact. Others arrested at home in similar circumstances have lost their homes and all their possessions.

Overcrowding

Overcrowding in prisons is a huge problem. To be crammed into a cell built for one person for thirteen hours, with a 'celly' who stinks because he hasn't showered for a week, can become intolerable!

Some guys watch rubbish television all night. Some people snore. Privacy is non-existent. There is the embarrassment of using the cell toilet which is not screened off. The general rule is: Wherever possible, use the toilet at night for one thing and not the other. However, if you have a bout of 'gastro', which is often rife in prison, you have no choice!

Many prisoners attempt to personalise their cells with photos of loved ones, posters of football teams, and often tasteless pictures of scantily-clad women. However a prisoner's cell is only a temporary abode. It is not personal space.

At any moment, staff can come into a cell, evict occupants and do a search. A prisoner can be required to change cells at any time without notice. He can arrive back at his cell to find he has a different cell mate, someone he has not met before and knows nothing about.

Overcrowding means that the facilities are overstretched and inadequate. It impacts on staff and prisoners, leading to aggravation that has the potential to create an explosive situation. The only way to keep a lid on it is to impose a harsher regime which is ultimately self-defeating.

Overcrowding means there is not enough work. To have several hundred people sitting around all day bored stiff is a recipe for disaster. The rehabilitative process breaks down.

Dehumanisation

When prisoners are admitted to prison, they are mandatorily strip-searched and have to exchange their own clothes for a drab uniform. Such dehumanising strategies force compliance with institutional regimes, eroding individual identities and rendering prisoners as 'non-people.'

During a prisoner's term inside, cells can be searched at any time, day or night. Pictures and photographs might be taken down and possessions dumped in a pile on the floor, where they may be damaged or go missing.

On one occasion, a prisoner got very agitated because his mug had gone missing. It was unclear whether it had been accidently broken or stolen. The prisoner was reprimanded for making such a fuss about something so minor. However, from his perspective, it was one of the few things that he actually owned.

Western society places huge emphasis on possessions and wealth as indicators of people's value and status. When a person is stripped of most of their possessions including, in some prisons, their first name, the little that they have left becomes very important.

Another dehumanising factor is the mindless boredom with which prisoners have to cope. This is compounded when there are not enough work tasks to keep prisoners occupied.

One ex-prisoner said:

> One of the reasons I avoid going back inside is that being inside is so bloody boringly awful that I reckon I would commit suicide.[1]

Burrows 407CF

Steve Burrows was in his late 30s when he first came into prison. He was escorted into reception to be processed.

The officer in charge shouted in his face:

'Name?'

'Steve Burrows.'

'No you're not! You're Burrows 407CF.'

Steve's possessions were then searched and he was required to submit to a demeaning strip search.

He said: 'I was humiliated.'

---

1 Jonathan Marshall, *How to Survive in the Nick* (London: Allison & Busby, 1974), 139.

The Invisible Man

Aprisoner attended a court hearing in America regarding the death sentence that had been pronounced upon him.
He said:

Though it was one hundred percent about me, and testimony was given by the prosecution and the defence, I never spoke nor was I asked to speak the whole time. But, who am I to speak? I am the invisible man. I'm poor, from an ethnic minority. The law deals with me as if I am faceless, voiceless, and anonymous. I am the invisible man.[1]

An ex-prisoner, writing about the dehumanising aspects of prison life, said:

Once a crim enters prison his actions are no longer perceived as those of a living, breathing human being. He enters as a criminal. His humanity and dignity are compromised insofar as he is perceived as, and treated by some as, a paedophile, or a murderer, or a drug dealer (or as invisible), rather than as a human being.[2]

---

1 'The Invisible Man', *Human Writes Newsletter*, 2011, 18.
2 Eddie Withnell, 'Stone Walls…The Spatial Determinations of the Criminal's Existential World' in *Australian Journal of Cultural Studies*, 2:2 (1984), 61.

Publicly Paraded

Dehumanising processes continue if a prisoner has to be taken out of prison into the public domain. At times, prisoners are paraded in chains through the public areas of hospitals. They are usually chained to beds, stretchers and wheelchair while under guard in hospital.

One prisoner discharged himself back to prison after major surgery because of the humiliation of being escorted while wearing restraints. He said: 'I would rather die in prison than continue being paraded about with a chain on like an animal.'

Obviously if a prisoner has to go to hospital, there is a need for security to decrease the risk of escape. However, procedures can be easily modified to be less humiliating — for example, the use of unobtrusive entrances, civilian clothes for security staff and minimal use of restraints.

When a prisoner is in hospital, and medical staff ask: 'What's he done?' confidentiality should apply. However, I know of situations where security staff have unethically revealed offence details. One hospitalised prisoner confided to me:

The screws told a nurse what I was in for. They shouldn't have done that. My treatment was fucking painful. Last time it wasn't. I don't think I'll go to the next appointment.

In Chains

Lord,
Prisoners are dehumanised in here,
as well as on the outside.
I am seeing another guy.
He is only allowed out of his cell
…when he is shackled in chains.

It's horrible to see a person
…chained up like an animal.
He has a chain around his waist,
to which his handcuffs are chained.
Chains on his ankles
…attached to the chains on his waist!
He clanks down the corridor
…all the way to the visitors' room.

Lord,
I know everyone in here has to be kept safe
…but this is ridiculous!
Over the top!
How many chains are needed to restrain a man?

Such treatment compromises humanity
…and dignity.

Lord, I can't change this man's circumstances,
but he seems glad to see me.
So, I will keep up my visits.

Sex

The lack of heterosexual relationships for adult prisoners is another dehumanising aspect of living behind bars. It causes tensions which may be channelled into violence, rape and other sordid practices.

One guy described an incident of rape:

> I was with a young bloke who got raped by a bloke who'd done sixteen or seventeen years. The bloke said to him, 'I know where your mother lives; I'll get her if you don't bend over'. Well the young fellow is only eighteen years old, just come to gaol, didn't know nothing, so he did what he was told.[1]

Sexual frustration contributes to high incidences of consensual sex between adult males in prison, most of whom would not normally participate in homosexual activity on the outside. It is common practice for condoms to be freely available in prisons as they reduce disease spread via body fluids.

---

1 Neer Korn, *Life Behind Bars: Conversations with Australian Male Inmates* (Sydney: New Holland Publishers, 2004),145.

Some prisoners make themselves available for 'blow jobs' and other sordid sexual services, receiving payment in tobacco or drugs.

Some prisoners ought to be allowed the privilege of sexual contact visits with their own partners. This would significantly decrease sexual tension and the violence that it can cause. It would also enable prisoners to maintain significant relationships which otherwise might flounder.

Media and Public Perceptions

Media attacks on people in prison can be relentless, reinforcing a perception that prisoners are a sub-species, not deserving of being treated as human. Media reports frequently manipulate facts, particularly exaggerating elements of violence or sex.

A newspaper editor, speaking as part of a television documentary, summed up his profession's approach as: 'All we are really interested in is a good story.'[1]

Following the death of a particularly notorious criminal, one newspaper announced: 'He is now in hell' and another described a photograph of a prisoner as: 'The face of pure evil'[2].

Typically, the general public knows nothing about prisoners except what appears in the media. This can reinforce presumptions that criminality is the sum total of a person's life. This is never the case. As one prisoner spelt it out: 'We are not all bad. I know I deserve to be in here but I am not all bad.'

When one gets to know prisoners, there is usually something good to say about each one, even those who have committed the most heinous crimes.

---

1   *Death Row*, Channel 4 TV, March 2012.
2   *Church Times*, 24 October 2003, 9.

Good and Evil

Many of us think of evil as a characteristic of a small group of people who are utterly unlike the rest of us. We demonise others to avoid the reality that there is bad in all of us. As Russian novelist and historian Alexander Solzhenitsyn wrote:

If only there were evil people insidiqusly committing evil deeds and it were necessary to separate the rest of us and destroy them. But the line dividing good and evil cuts through the heart of every human being, and who is willing to destroy a piece of his own heart?[1]

---

1   Alexander Solzhenitsyn, *The Gulag Archipelago 1918–1956* (USA: Harper & Row, 1973).

Protection

There are protection units in most prisons. These house prisoners who would be at risk in mainstream areas. Protected prisoners have often received high profile media attention as a result of crimes such as sex offences and extreme violence against children.

In prisons, there are always bullies waiting to take advantage of people who appear vulnerable, for whatever reason. Mental illnesses and other idiosyncratic behaviours can put some prisoners at risk in mainstream. Young prisoners may be at risk from predators because of boyish or effeminate appearances. Elderly prisoners in poor health are often placed in protection.

Protected prisoners live under constant threat of serious assault, even murder. There are instances where protected prisoners have been badly beaten, stabbed, had boiling water thrown over them, or been set alight after being doused with flammable liquid.

Protection units are not the place to be unless it is absolutely necessary. Once there, prisoners are stigmatised and labelled as 'dogs', because of the nature of their offences or because they have 'grassed up' (informed on) other prisoners or associates.

Protection units are 'prisons within prisons'.

Following the Murder of a Child

Lord God,
I am going to see John again today.
He is in isolation,
at risk of assault or worse, if he were placed among other prisoners.
He was convicted of murdering a child.

I didn't know what to expect,
the first time I went to see him.
He'd been written up by the media as a monster.
All the usual rubbish, half-truths, untruths,
inflating gruesome details.
I don't know how they get away with it.
I really don't.

Lord!
The media does dehumanise people like John,
referring to him only as 'the killer' or 'the murderer.'
Others are described only as 'paedophiles'
or 'drug dealers.'
No-one stops to think that they are
really human beings.

But Lord God,
John is just an ordinary kind of guy
Who got into some really bad stuff.
When people ask me what John is like
(and they will!)
I'll always say: 'He's just like anyone else,
a human being,
…except he tragically committed a terrible crime.'

Lord,
You know, better than me,
John's crime is not the whole story of his life.
He has to take responsibility,
for what he's done.
He will suffer the consequences
for the rest of his life,
however long that will be.
And yes Lord, he is suffering!

I can't make excuses for him,
but I suspect his past,
over which he had little control,
has impacted negatively
and contributed to what he has done.

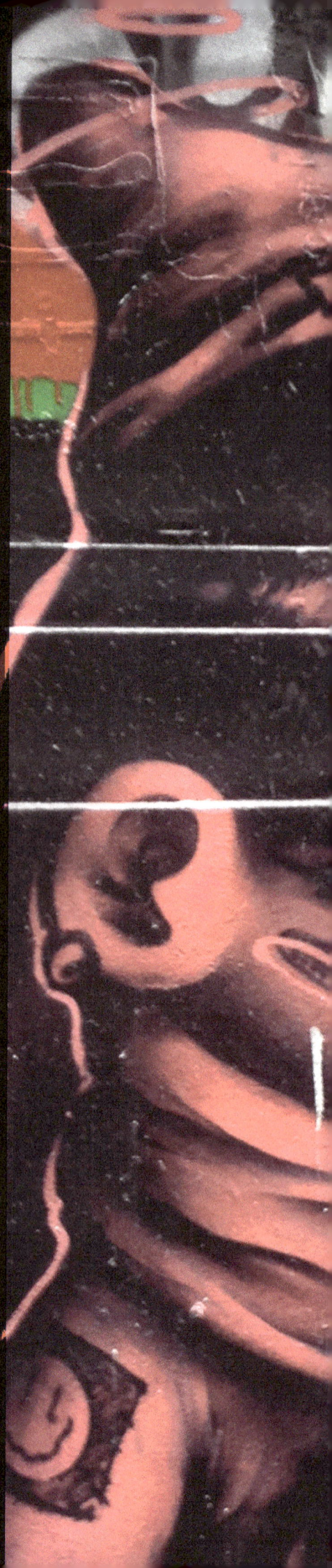

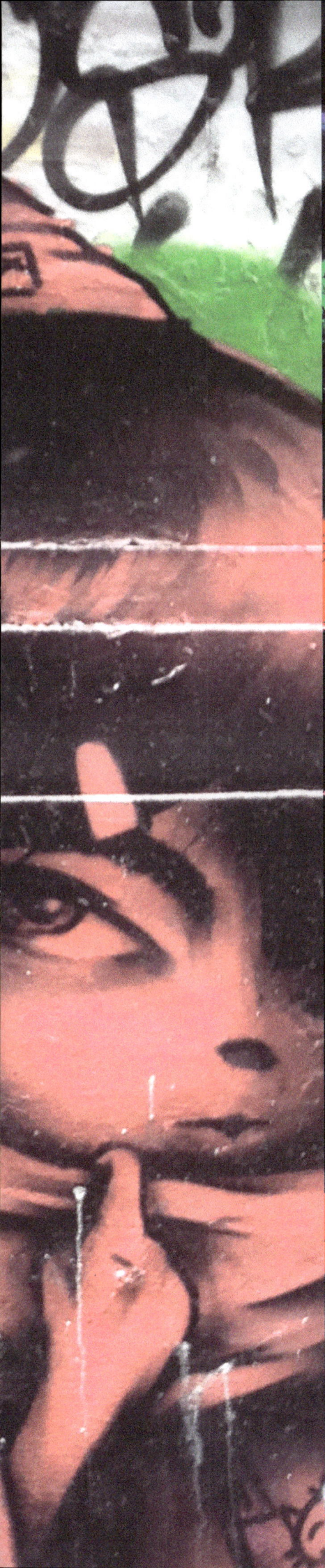

I know that some of the prison officers,
who have young children of their own,
would like to give him a kicking.
Yes, Lord, I heard them talking about it.
It might happen when no responsible person is
    around.
I fear it will just make things worse.

Lord,
He can't be kept in isolation forever.
He will end up in the unit for protected
    prisoners,
but sooner or later the others are likely to get
    at him
…with a 'shiv,'
…. give him a kicking,
…or even kill him.

John is apprehensive about his future.
To put it bluntly Lord,
he's 'shit scared.'
He might kill himself, or try to.
I and others will try to persuade him
    otherwise,
but if he's determined
…eventually
…it will happen.
He can't be watched 24/7 forever.

I've not yet spoken to him
about Jesus and the resurrection,
but when it seems the right time,
I will tell him that there is nothing
that anyone has ever done
that You will not forgive,
provided there is genuine remorse
and commitment to change

Lord,
I pray that this man might survive
…the next 24 hours.

Violence

The potential for violence in prisons is ever-present. People who work in prisons need to be calm, but at the same time alert to the risks of making themselves vulnerable. If there is a need to call for 'the cavalry' (back up support), this increases the chances of someone getting hurt.

Simple safety precautions include maintaining access to doors and arranging the furniture to avoid being trapped. Most prisons require all staff members to carry duress alarms which summon rapid assistance in the case of threats and emergencies. In some facilities, civilian staff are offered unarmed defence combat training to equip them to fend off an attack.

Vicious, unprovoked attacks on staff members are rare, but they do happen. Such occurrences inevitably raise tensions and increase mistrust. A typical response is for 'lockdowns' to be put in place, resulting in prisoners being confined to designated areas for an extended time. This can include non-violent prisoners and those who were not involved in security breaches.

There are always prisoners who manufacture weapons, mainly (as they see it) for self-protection, but sometimes to prepare for an act of revenge. It is possible to manufacture a weapon from almost anything. For example, a ball point pen can be lethal if plunged into an eye or soft tissue. Similarly, a nail with a manufactured handle attached can do a lot of damage. There are numerous ways to make a 'shiv' (a slang term for any sharp implement used as a knife-like weapon). Prisoners simply need to find a piece of hard material, grind it down to a cutting edge or point, put a handle on it and they have a lethal weapon. (One attitude I have heard is *'If my enemy knows I have a weapon he may not attack. If I know my enemy is armed, I may not attack.'*)

'Grassing Up'

A big issue for mainstream prisoners is the extent to which they should report violence (sexual or otherwise) against themselves. If a prisoner makes a report, the first question will be: 'Do you want this to go any further?' If a complaint goes further, and the perpetrator is charged, word will get around. The victim will be labelled as a 'dog', guilty of 'grassing up'. This places the victim at risk of more violence and even their families on the outside becoming targets for retaliation.

If someone is labelled in this way, they are almost always forced into protection. So typically, prisoners prefer to explain away their injuries: 'I fell out of the top bunk' or 'I tripped and fell down the stairs.' In prison, the first priority is survival.

Most staff do a good job and give whatever support they can to those in their care. However, at times, physical and psychological violence is dished out by staff toward prisoners. One prisoner recounted his experience of being 'taken down the back', to an isolated punishment cell. He said:

> They threw me into the cell and got stuck into me, kicking, hitting me with batons, mainly body blows so that there are no obvious wounds. I couldn't stand up when they left. They called me 'a piece of shit' and left me in isolation for three days until I was able to appear 'normal.' They knew I wouldn't complain. No point in complaining. They will only do it again.

Psychological Violence

The word goes round to a number of staff: 'We are going to give this guy a hard time.' This might include calling a prisoner for a visit only when the visiting time has actually started, cutting down the time with family by at least twenty minutes.

Sometimes, prisoners miss important medical and dental treatment because unit staff have failed to allow time to get to appointments. Another appointment time might not be available for weeks. If a prisoner has had a toothache for a week and now has to wait another two before he can see a dentist, this could trigger anger and violence. From time to time, letters 'get delayed' or 'go missing.' Interference with mail can be hard for prisoners to take, especially when holding out for letters from partners and families.

Staff might provoke a prisoner to commit an offence for which he is sent to a punishment cell or charged. Another abusive practice is to place a disliked and vulnerable prisoner in a cell with a prisoner who is known to be violent. On one occasion, I visited a prisoner in hospital who had been subject to extreme violence from his 'celly'. He would never fully recover from his injuries and should never have been put in the same cell as his assailant.

Punishment Cell

Describing his experiences in a punishment cell, Gordon said:

That officer has been fucking me about for days. He still hasn't got my phone numbers on the system so I can ring my missus. She'll be worried. She was expecting a call yesterday. I worry about her and the kids, whether she's coping. In the end, I told him to fuck off and ended up here. It's doing my head in. Given half a chance, I will kill the bastard.

Self-harm

'Slashing up' or, more seriously, attempted suicide is often a cry for help. One prisoner said that he had put in several requests for an appointment at the medical centre because he was anxious about his eyes:

> They just ignore me. They don't give shit about us. I'll be fucking blind before I get an appointment. I cut the end of my finger off so that when the staff see the blood they will have to take me to the medical centre. Then, I can ask about my eyes.

Another prisoner who had been a 'slasher' for years explained:

> It takes me out of myself. I feel better about things when I slash up. I don't know why. It only lasts a few days.

Suicide in prison tends to have a chilling effect on most other prisoners and staff, especially those who know the person concerned. It can happen accidentally when the intention is only to self-harm. Again, it starts out as a cry for help. It can be a knee-jerk reaction to a particular situation, or carefully planned. Those most at risk are people serving very long sentences who can no longer see any point in living.

Death by Hanging

Lord,
Another suicide,
not totally unexpected.
Ritchie had been in prison
more than 15 years.
The prospect of him ever being released
was not good.

I got to know him quite well
…over the years.
He was usually willing to chat,
when I saw him at work or in his unit.

He would talk about most things,
but nothing to do with faith
…not you, Lord;
…nor Jesus and the resurrection;
…nor religious belief.
Who knows why?
Only you, Lord.

He could be quite kind,
helping semi-literate guys to read or write
…personal letters,
…communication with lawyers,
…reading fliers on notice boards.

Lord,
Over the years the media,
…and others
…inside and out,
have had a field day
…dehumanising
…and vilifying.

Now that he is dead,
headlines appear: 'Killer now in hell.'
But, no-one knows
what transpired between you, Lord and him,
if anything,
during his last night
in the hours before
…he killed himself.

State-Sanctioned Violence

State-sanctioned violence, including death penalties for those who have committed premeditated murder, still seems to have wide support.

A significant number of 'lifers' have said to me that they wish the death sentence were applicable to them. They believed that death would be preferable to spending 20 to 30 years in prison.

The debate about the death penalty continues.

The most barbaric and dehumanising application of the death penalty in a so-called civilised society is in the USA. I have been corresponding with a man who has been on death row for 14 years. His latest stay of execution was granted two and a half hours before his appointed time. This is as bad as psychological and emotional violence can get.

An inmate on death row expressed in poetry a preference to spend eternity in hell, rather than continue in his present circumstances:

I AM READY TO CALL IT QUITS. PACK UP AND GO TO THE ONE BELOW. LIFE IS TRULY A LIVING HELL I WISH TO CLOSE MY EYES, TO SLEEP THE ENDLESS SLEEP, TO BE WITH THE ONE BELOW, FOR MY SOUL HE MAY KEEP.

I HAVE LIVED MY LIFE TO THE BEST OF MY ABILITY, YET WHERE DO I RESIDE? AT THIS DAMNED FACILITY. I'M LIVING THE SLOW DEATH, ONE HOUR AT A TIME, LOCKED IN THIS HELLISH CAGE, NO BIGGER THAN SIX BY NINE.

AT LEAST WITH THE ONE BELOW, I KNOW WHERE I STAND, FOR WHEN ONE PLAYS WITH FIRE, THEY SHALL BURN THEIR HAND. CONFLICTED OR NOT, THIS IS HOW IT MUST BE. AN ETERNITY SPENT WITH THE ONE BELOW. NOW THAT'S DEFINITELY FOR ME.[1]

---

1   Lupo S Wolf, *Human Writes* (Summer 2013), 15. Used with permission.

Medical Treatment

Many medical practitioners will not work in prison hospitals because of fear. In reality, there is more chance of being assaulted in a public hospital than in a prison. Most people in prison are grateful for medical treatment and there are some wonderful, caring staff who treat their patients with sensitivity.

Unfortunately there are also exceptions. Some practitioners treat prisoners with disdain, denying them a fair hearing and providing only the bare minimum standard of care. As one prison hospital inmate put it: 'That nurse treats us like shit.'

The turnover of medics in prison hospitals is alarming. This is mainly due to overwork, scarce resources and difficulties in recruiting staff. One prison doctor said to me:

However good you are at your job, and however committed you are to making a difference to the lives of people, you wake up one morning and think, 'I can't put up with this shit any longer', and you resign. That's what I am doing today.

Reinforcing Their Power

If prison officers are confident in their own power, they do not need to show it. It is only those who really lack confidence to do their job humanely who feel they have to keep reinforcing their 'power profile'.

An occupational hazard of working in prisons is the development of an attitude of superiority. Criminologists call this the 'prisonisation of staff'. In part, it results from viewing prisoners as commodities to work with, rather than human beings deserving of respect.

Staff can use a range of strategies to ensure they are proactive in providing the best possible care. They can facilitate mail going in and out as quickly as possible and ensure that prisoners get to visits and medical appointments in plenty of time. Potential conflict can be dissipated by acting wisely and with discretion. Allowances sometimes need to be made for prisoners who are having a particularly difficult time due to health issues, anxiety about court appearances, or family crises. Staff should be trustworthy and able to deal firmly but tactfully with prisoners.

Throwing the First Stone

We all share the same humanity — for better or worse. Thinking about those who have done wrong and how they should be treated, I am reminded of a story in The Bible.

Authorities brought a woman to Jesus who had been caught in the act of adultery — a crime for which the punishment in those days was death by stoning. They said to Jesus: 'This woman was caught in the very act of committing adultery. Now in the law Moses commanded us to stone such women. Now what do you say?'

Jesus did not answer them immediately. The life of this woman was in the balance. Eventually, he said: 'Let anyone among you who is without sin be the first to throw a stone at her.'

No doubt there was a pregnant silence. Perhaps the expectation was that someone would shove the woman into a pit dug in readiness for the stoning, and then throw the first stone. But, one by one, starting with the most important of them, those who had brought the accusation walked off.

A Crazy Place to Work

Surviving in prison is a challenge for the staff as well as the prisoners. The majority of civilian staff, such as nurses, social workers, psychologists and educators, do not spend most of their career working in prisons. The day-to-day confrontation with intractable problems in an unpredictable and stressful environment can take a toll.

A psychologist described the never-ending pressure to see numerous clients as 'crazy':

> The list just gets longer and longer. At the end of many days, I have more clients on the list than I had when I started. We need more staff because mental health and prisons are at the bottom of the list when it comes to providing adequate resources. We are always short-staffed. In private practice, I can control my list of clients and spend time doing things other than face-to-face counselling.

Many uniformed staff members do make careers of working in prisons. They get several months of good initial training and ongoing professional development when they are in post. There are opportunities for promotion. They enjoy camaraderie with colleagues, as well as advocacy and support from their union. In addition, their working day tends to be more structured.

Survival Tips for Prisoners

There is an old adage, 'If you can't do the time, don't do the crime.' Some prisoners do their time more easily than others. They walk into prison to be greeted by friends and relatives who will show them the ropes and guide them through their initial orientation. Sometimes there are three generations of the same family in prison—grandfather, father, son and maybe brothers and cousins. However, being in prison is a horrible experience for most people, especially the first time. Prisoners spend their time in a locked institution with people with whom they would not normally choose to associate, some of whom have committed the most appalling crimes.

Over the years, I have had the opportunity to gather up tips and advice from prisoners who have 'done the time', been released, reoffended and returned to gaol on more than one occasion. (One of my 'advisers' had more than 20 admissions!) Sadly, the social dynamics of the prison system are such that there are always predators on the prowl looking for weaknesses in other inmates, ready to take advantage of anyone, especially 'new guys'. It really is the law of the jungle, the survival of the fittest.

- Do not show emotion as it might be interpreted as weakness. There will be many occasions when you feel like crying. Save it up and cry into your pillow at night. Nights are the worst time for missing family, home and friends. Sometimes when you wake up, you don't immediately know where you are. Then you remember you are in prison. It can hit you like a ton of bricks.

- Avoid confrontations where possible. However, you might be cornered and threatened by violence if you do not comply with demands such as: 'Do this' or 'Give me that'. The only way to deal with this sort of aggression is to refuse, stand your ground. If the bully gets what he wants, he will be back for more—frequently. Also, if you allow someone to disrespect you in front of others, it will mark you out as weak and incite others to harass you. The probability is that when the bully knows you will resist regardless of the outcome, he will tend to go for other 'prey' he knows will be more compliant. Others, too, will note your resistance. It is better stand firm and risk a beating than to become a target for persistent harassment.

- Mind your own business. If you see someone being assaulted or bullied in any way, walk away. Don't make it your problem. Don't get involved—otherwise, you will likely become the next victim. Above all, do not tell prison staff or call on them to intervene. If you do, you will be labelled as a 'dog', a 'grass'. If that occurs, you will be shunned by other prisoners, or seriously assaulted or even killed. Even if you are moved to another unit or prison, your reputation as a 'grass' will go with you via the grapevine. If you get out of gaol and then return, you will still be a 'dog'.

- Don't pry. If other prisoners want you to know why they are in prison, they will tell you. Don't ask about other prisoners' families, visitors or mail.

- Walk with your head held up so that predators do not perceive you as afraid, uncertain or vulnerable. On the other hand, never 'eyeball' others—someone will demand: 'What the fuck are you looking at?' Trouble will usually follow.

- Never allow other inmates to know personal details such as your home address, telephone numbers or the names of those close to you. A prisoner, or someone on the outside, might make trouble for them in order to get at you. This can include dodgy phone calls, attempts at blackmail to get them to pay your debts or bring drugs into the prison, burglary, assault or property damage.

- Don't take drugs because you don't know what's in them. Accepting drugs in prison leads to all sorts of complications, especially if you can't pay for them. To be in debt to others in prison is a recipe for disaster — it might result in your family being attacked or you being moved into protection.

One pitfall is for prisoners to 'secrete' prescribed medications to trade for other things. They swallow down medications for the mandatory 'mouth check' but then vomit it up. Jimmy warned:

I started trading my medication for tobacco. It went into a drug pool where it was mixed and sold on. When I tried to stop doing it, they threatened to bash me. I eventually stopped, but it was difficult. I wished I had never started.

- Take prescribed medications. In most cases, they will help you cope better in prison.

- Be aware that one way to get protection, without being placed in a protection unit, is to be taken under the wing of an individual or group within the prison. However, they usually want something in return for their protection such as 'sexual favours'. The protector might 'loan you out' in lieu of a debt or as payment for drugs, tobacco, a radio or television. If you are under group protection, this might mean that you are expected to deliver sexual favours to several members or the whole group.

- Gangs and other groups within prisons tend to look after their own. There may be indigenous or tribal groups, bike gangs or individuals who simply gel into some kind of solidarity to look out for each other. If you are able to join such a group, and the conditions of belonging are not too onerous, it is best to opt in. It will guarantee a measure of protection. Individual predators will think twice about having a go at an individual if it means messing with a whole group.

- Don't view the prison staff as enemies. Establish a pattern of positive interaction with them by showing respect without becoming an obvious favourite. Remember, it is not their fault you are in prison. Most of them are just doing their job as well as they can. They have their bad days too. 'Please' and 'thank you' go a long way in enabling you to have a positive working relationship with most staff. Don't be constantly 'in their face' with trivial requests. Overcrowding means they are bombarded with far more than they can realistically manage. As far as possible, be compliant because you might as well retain privileges such as having a television, getting access to recreation and having visitors. In the long run, you cannot beat the system, so why bang your head against a brick wall? All you will get is a headache.

- Nurture your relationships on the outside. Take action to ensure that family ties are not broken. Letters and phone calls keep you in touch. Regular visits by family and friends are important but not always practical and affordable, especially if the prison is located in an isolated area and visitors have to use public transport. It can also be difficult for parents with small children. Some visitors find the admission and security procedures irritating and humiliating.

- Remember, family and friends on the outside have to get on with their lives with working, paying the bills and getting the kids to school. Don't be too demanding. During a phone call, swearing at your partner will do nothing to encourage support. In fact, it might be used as an opportunity to break off a relationship with you.

- Avoid prison tattoos and used needles. Hepatitis and other blood-borne infections can occur. Steer clear of 'brews' (alcoholic drink concocted by prisoners from anything they can lay their hands on) — they could be poisonous.

- When your time to be released or transferred to minimum security is approaching, watch out for people who may have a grudge against you. They may try to provoke you to violence, or some other misdemeanour, so that your move will be cancelled.

- Get involved in positive activities, education and sport. Joining a unit football team is a good way to foster group camaraderie. It is also a good protection strategy. If you are a good player and the men in the unit want you on their team, they will look after you. Keep fit and work out. If you are seen working out with tough guys, prospective predators will think twice about attacking you. Positive activities make time pass more quickly and also make you feel a lot better about yourself. Make friends slowly and carefully. Suss them out. Ask yourself: 'Is this guy genuine or trying to con me?'

- Help others in situations where there is no 'comeback'. If you are literate, you may be able to help other prisoners to write or read their mail, fill in forms or explain variations in prison rules that have appeared on a notice board.

- Check out what is on offer in the prison chapel. A significant number of prisoners attend the worship services, Bible studies and a range of growth courses offered by chaplains. Some receive teaching from religious visitors such as an imam, rabbi, Jehovah's Witness and others. Many attend these gatherings because it is a bit different from their usual routine. For a start, it is voluntary. You attend because you want to, not because you have to. Some prisoners will have ulterior motives for attending (such as getting into the tea, coffee and biscuits after the service!) For others, it becomes a meeting place with mates who have been moved to different parts of the prison. Some come to chapel to do drug deals. Regardless of the motivation, some hear and feel things that change their lives. Many prisoners keep participating in religious activities, even if they started off with a wrong motive.

- Attend Alcoholics Anonymous (AA) or Narcotics Anonymous (NA), if you need to do so. These meetings provide a change in routine from the mindless boredom that goes with living in prison. They are also an opportunity to better yourself and improve your chances of doing more than just surviving on the outside.

Positive Outcomes

If a prisoner is mentally strong and physically robust, he can make use of time in prison for his own benefit. Indeed, there can be positive gains. After all, the prison experience is supposed to be rehabilitative.

If people come into prison illiterate or only partly literate, and then learn to read and write, the way they see the world upon release is very different.

At the other end of the academic spectrum, some prisoners serving longer sentences will be able to settle down and apply themselves to study for a university degree. On one occasion, the chancellor of a university came to a prison dressed in his academic regalia and presented a prisoner with his degree. It was a positive moment within the life of our community.

Learning a trade such as bricklaying can be invaluable once a person is released. It gives him a start on a building site. Eventually these skills can enable a prisoner to earn a good living — the kind of success that leads to confidence and making the grade on the outside.

Some people take the opportunity to start (or restart) attendance at AA or NA, giving themselves the opportunity to be 'clean' by the time they are released.

A positive outcome of imprisonment for some is the discovery of hidden talents such as painting, drawing, woodwork, metalwork and cooking. Some prisons host arts and crafts exhibitions to which the public is invited. Art sales can give prisoners a source of income and motivation to stay out of prison.

For some, the discovery of spiritual and religious dimensions of life while in prison can be transformative. For most, this is not immediate and dramatic but rather a gradual awareness that there might be some substance in 'the God thing'. Perhaps there is something or someone 'out there'.

Discovery of spirituality while in prison almost always begins by seeing faith in action in others — prisoners or staff. One prisoner said of a lay chaplain:

He didn't just talk the talk — he walked the walk too. He had a reputation of following things through. When he said he would do something he did it — you could rely on him. He was a man of his word, a man of action. It was his tireless efforts to seek justice for me and comfort me in times of despair and desperation that kept me from the brink of self-destruction.

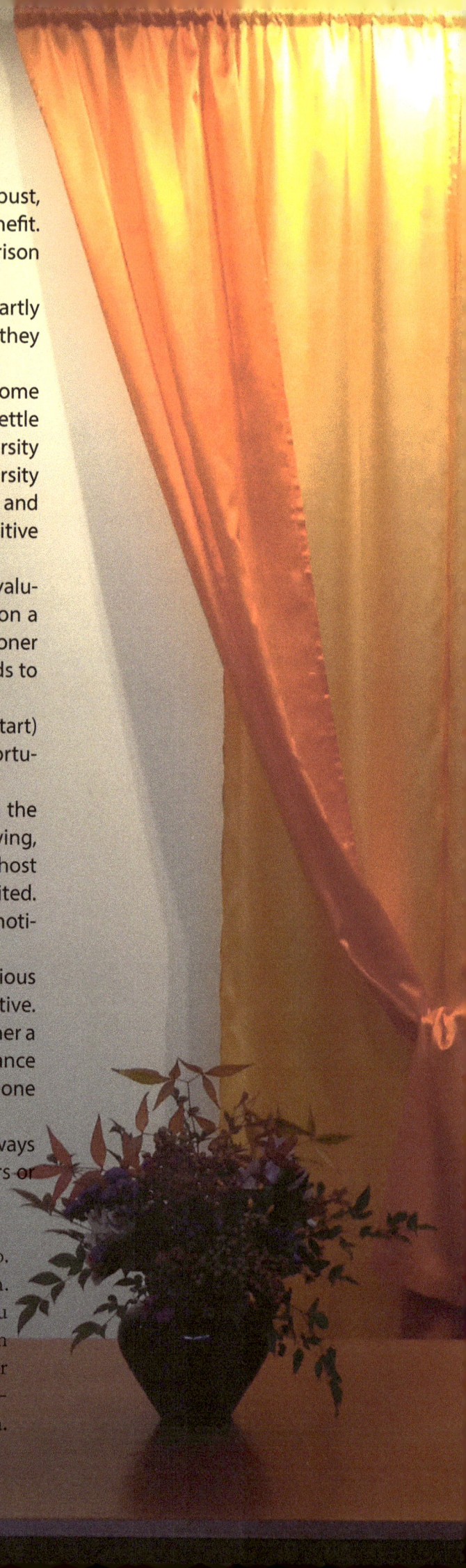

Sunday, Again

Following the Death of a Prisoner

Lord God,
When I woke up this morning,
I couldn't believe it's Sunday again!
They seem to come around so quickly!

As you know,
I don't feel great after a hard week.
The funeral was very difficult, as they are
…after a sudden, unexpected death.
Barney was only 30.

It seems as if it was an accidental overdose.
But we won't know for sure for weeks.

All those traumatised people,
some will never get over it,
especially, his parents
…his brothers and sisters.

Some of the younger guys in here
have taken it very hard,
especially those who looked up to Barney.
They saw him as a leader and mentor.
Sometime this week,
we will have a gathering in the gym,
for the guys who want to come.

We will have a photo of Barney.
Light a candle for him.
Those who want to speak about him will get their chance.
Then, we will commend him to you,
and pray for his family.

Lord,
As always,
but especially this week,
those who come to chapel,
need to hear the Good News of Jesus and his resurrection.

There's not a lot of good news in here.
Most of the news is bad.
Death, long sentences, violence, fear, fights, abuse,
mental illness and drugs.
From a human point of view, it's a bit of a nightmare.

Lord,
To know you are here
(and involved),
makes a huge difference.
I wouldn't be able to cope
without this knowledge and conviction.

CHAPTER 3

DRUGS & ALCOHOL

Bird Under Arrest

A pigeon was in custody after smuggling drugs into a high security prison. The bird raised suspicions after four prisoners appeared to be stoned shortly after the bird landed on a ledge next to a cell window. Drugs, stuffed into tiny bags, were attached to the pigeon's legs. After its arrest, the bird was kept in a prisoner's cell as a pet while police carried out investigations.

Drug Use in the Community

A senior police officer observed that illicit drugs were 'in every community, in every high school. Illicit drugs impact directly on anti-social behaviour, crime rates, assaults and thefts.'

A significant number of prisoners are living with various addictions when they come to prison. Sadly, some are born with addictions transferred to them in the womb by mothers who consumed alcohol and other harmful drugs while pregnant.

Substance abuse is not simply the result of an initial choice to use alcohol or drugs. Poor quality of life is a big factor in things getting out of hand with risky behaviour and habit formation. Some people get lured in: 'It's nice to be out of it with no worries.' This might be due to depression and believing, 'It helps me cope better.' An alcoholic who always has an alcoholic drink next to his bed observed 'I need a drink first thing in the morning before I can do anything'.

I am certainly sympathetic to this point of view as a result of my own experiences of depression. I have had moments when I have reached for a bottle, hoping it would increase my capacity to cope. On one occasion, just before I had to conduct a funeral with nearly 400 people in attendance, I took a generous swig out of a sherry bottle. And it did help — but only for a couple of hours!

Sometimes people get mixed up in alcohol and drug abuse as a result of peer pressure. ('Come on, try it! Everyone else is. Use this … take that … and life will be much better.') Life can become increasingly complicated when psychological, emotional, and physical dependence on drugs and alcohol increases. Addictive behaviour certainly influences people's choices and severely impacts on their life options.

Drug Use in Prison

Approximately 70 percent of prisoners are 'inside' for offences involving illegal drugs — importing, exporting, manufacturing, trafficking, possessing or using.

Prison intelligence is crucial in trying to stem the flow of drugs. Tip-offs can be gleaned from letters, phone calls and the histories of some inmates. A few prisoners will take the risk of providing information to staff. Prison staff will make unannounced searches. In spite of all this, as well as sniffer dogs and electronic monitoring, drugs still get into prisons.

Bringing Drugs In

The availability of drugs in prisons is a significant cause of bullying. Brian approached me:

> I want to speak to you in confidence. Things are bad. I need help. You saw me when I came in and you know this is my first time in the adult prison. I am in for drug use and dealing. Two blokes in my unit say that I have to get my missus to bring drugs in for them or they will get someone on the outside to burn our house down with her and the kids in it.

Not an empty threat; such are the dynamics of prison. I had to deal with this situation without disclosing that Brian had 'grassed up' two bullies, or else he would have been placed in protection. I was able to have a quiet word with someone in authority. The bullies were split up and transferred to other prisons, without being told the real reason for their moves.

Unusually Unhealthy

The impact of drug use is significant in terms of medical and physical issues. Even marijuana, sometimes referred to as a 'soft drug', undoubtedly poses major health risks. Many prisoners come into prison looking gaunt and unwell from excessive substance use. Their food is usually unhealthy and lacking in nutrition. While in prison, drug intake is usually suspended or reduced, and the amount of nutritious food is increased. When people leave prison, they have usually put on weight and experience improvements in health. However, it is not uncommon for them to return, a few weeks or months later, once again looking gaunt and unwell. As this cycle continues over a number of years, general health gradually deteriorates and life expectancy is significantly reduced.

Keeping Me Alive

Phil made good use of his prison terms to get off drugs for periods of time. He was of average height and addicted to heroin. He described himself as:

> About eight stone, battleship grey with the high cheekbones of an addict, matted hair, probably the same jeans on for about a month. I didn't care about myself, never mind anyone else.

The only way Phil could regulate his drug use was by being arrested:

> I would go shoplifting which would either help me to get money for more drugs, or it would get me back to prison. Prison would keep me alive. Any time I was at death's door I would go there and have a drying out period.

So Addicted It's Not Funny

A female prisoner wrote:

> I began smoking cigarettes and pot when I was 14. I also drank on occasions when I could get away with it. I am now 31 and an all-day pot smoker. I also used to be a drinker but, after having a seizure from drinking, I had to quit.
>
> Today I ran out of pot. As soon as I am out of pot, I am cranky, moody, mean, short-tempered. The list goes on. It is making me sick to type this as I have spent years and years of my life yearning for a high instead of living.
>
> I have horrible short-term memory. I have no appetite unless I smoke. I don't sleep well without it and have severe withdrawal symptoms when I don't have it.
>
> I always told myself that I wasn't addicted, that it's what I want to do; but in reality, I see, now that I am so addicted, that it's not funny. I literally feel sick when I don't have it.

I am not looking forward to the long road ahead. I don't have any coping skills as I have only used pot, cigs and alcohol to deal with the stress of life.

I hope that my story will help someone else.

I don't want to lose my family but I will if I can't change my ways. To see the hurt in my husband's eyes is enough for me.

Just to Cope

William's drug addiction led to his conviction for fraud. He said:

I used to socialise with a group of people who used drugs once or twice a week in a recreational way, at a party or a night club. I earned plenty of money so I could indulge without financial hardship. Then pressure at work increased, long hours and quite a bit of travel, things were not great with our marriage. I started to use, to give me a boost when I was tired out, and it gradually increased to a point where I needed some every day just to cope. The rest is history. Here I am.

Desperate

Craig had a long history of drug dependence. He said:

I know I shouldn't be back in prison but things got difficult out there. I couldn't get regular work so we were always behind with the rent. The owner kept threatening to kick us out. My partner was smoking pot so she was 'out of it' a lot of the time. We were harassed by dealers who kept coming round. I did some coke to ease the pressure, woke up one day, no food in the house, no money, no drugs and owing the dealer. I was desperate. I went and did a robbery at a shop masked up and carrying a weapon. I wasn't going to use it. It was only to frighten people. The woman in there freaked out before I said anything. So I grabbed some money out of the till and scarpered. Eventually, the coppers caught up with me and here I am, again. They've charged me with armed robbery this time, so I could be in for a long one.

Wiping Out Brain Cells

Frank was eleven years old when he started smoking marijuana. His family had a few acres of land in an isolated area and they had grown it ever since Frank could remember, mainly for personal use with a bit of wheeling and dealing on the side. Occasionally, a visitor would arrive, usually after dark, and depart carrying a full sack.

By the age of 14, when Frank left home, smoking pot was normal for him. That's when the trouble started. No longer having a reliable source of the drug, he had to start buying it on the streets. It wasn't difficult to get, but it was expensive. He soon found out, the only way to guarantee a regular supply was to sign up as a dealer. With a profit margin, Frank was now able to feed his habit. Occasionally, he would add something to bulk it out, usually a small amount of cheap tobacco.

Frank received two warnings from the police about what would happen if he persisted with this 'business'. The third time, he was arrested, warned again and released. The fourth time he was sentenced to a spell in a juvenile detention centre where, as part of an education package, he was offered the chance to participate in a programme to help him kick the habit. However, Frank liked smoking pot and couldn't see any reason why he shouldn't continue.

By the time Frank was 19, he was in an adult prison for the second time. He remained dismissive of attempts to educate him about the long-term negative effects of drug use. In 'prison-speak', prolonged drug use could affect his head and 'start wiping out his brain cells'. Frank was undeterred. He had never felt better. He enjoyed using marijuana and he could make money. His mantra was: 'If I have to do a bit of gaol, it's not too bad. Some of my mates are always in here anyway.'

I AM CRYSTAL 'METH'

I DESTROY HOMES, I TEAR FAMILIES APART,
TAKE YOUR CHILDREN AND THAT'S JUST THE START.
I'M MORE COSTLY THAN DIAMONDS, MORE PRECIOUS THAN GOLD,
THE SORROW I BRING IS A SIGHT TO BEHOLD.
IF YOU NEED ME I'M EASILY FOUND,
I LIVE ALL AROUND IN SCHOOLS AND IN TOWNS.
I LIVE WITH THE RICH, I LIVE WITH THE POOR,
I LIVE DOWN THE STREET AND MAYBE NEXT DOOR.
I'M MADE IN A LAB BUT NOT LIKE YOU THINK,
I CAN BE MADE UNDER THE KITCHEN SINK,
IN YOUR CHILD'S CLOSET AND EVEN THE WOODS.
IF THIS SCARES YOU TO DEATH WELL IT CERTAINLY SHOULD.
I HAVE MANY NAMES BUT ONE YOU KNOW BEST,
I'M SURE YOU HAVE HEARD OF ME,
MY NAME IS CRYSTAL METH.
MY POWER IS AWESOME. TRY ME & YOU'LL SEE,
BUT IF YOU DO YOU MAY NEVER BREAK FREE.
JUST TRY ME ONCE AND I MIGHT LET YOU GO,
BUT TRY ME TWICE AND I'LL OWN YOUR SOUL.
WHEN I POSSESS YOU, YOU'LL STEAL AND YOU'LL LIE,
YOU'LL DO WHAT YOU HAVE TO JUST TO GET HIGH.
THE CRIMES YOU'LL COMMIT FOR MY NARCOTIC CHARMS
WILL BE WORTH THE PLEASURE YOU'LL FEEL IN YOUR ARMS.
YOU'LL LIE TO YOUR MOTHER, YOU'LL STEAL FROM YOUR DAD,
WHEN YOU SEE THEIR TEARS YOU SHOULD FEEL SAD.
BUT YOU'LL FORGET YOUR MORALS AND HOW YOU WERE RAISED,
I'LL BE YOUR CONSCIENCE, I'LL TEACH YOU MY WAYS.
I TAKE KIDS FROM PARENTS AND PARENTS FROM KIDS,
TURN PEOPLE FROM GOD AND SEPARATE FRIENDS.
I'LL TAKE EVERYTHING FROM YOU, YOUR LOOKS AND YOUR PRIDE,

I'LL BE WITH YOU ALWAYS, RIGHT BY YOUR SIDE.
YOU'LL GIVE UP EVERYTHING; YOUR FAMILY YOUR HOME,
YOUR FRIENDS, YOUR MONEY THEN YOU'LL BE ALONE.
I'LL TAKE AND I'LL TAKE TILL YOU'VE NOTHING TO GIVE.
WHEN I'M FINISHED WITH YOU, YOU'LL BE LUCKY TO LIVE.
IF YOU TRY ME BE WARNED THIS IS NO GAME,
IF GIVEN THE CHANCE, I'LL DRIVE YOU INSANE.
I'LL RAVISH YOUR BODY, I'LL CONTROL YOUR MIND,
I'LL OWN YOU COMPLETELY — YOUR SOUL WILL BE MINE.
THE NIGHTMARES I'LL GIVE YOU WHILE LYING IN BED,
THE VOICES YOU HEAR FROM INSIDE YOUR HEAD,
THE SWEATS AND THE SHAKES, THE VISIONS YOU'LL SEE,
I WANT YOU TO KNOW THEY ARE ALL GIFTS FROM ME.
BUT THEN IT'S TOO LATE AND YOU'LL KNOW IN YOUR HEART
THAT YOU ARE MINE AND WE SHALL NOT PART.
YOU'LL REGRET THAT YOU TRIED ME — THEY ALWAYS DO,
BUT REMEMBER YOU CAME TO ME NOT I TO YOU.
YOU KNEW THIS WOULD HAPPEN, MANY TIMES YOU WERE TOLD,
BUT YOU CHALLENGED MY POWER AND CHOSE TO BE BOLD.
YOU COULD HAVE SAID NO AND JUST WALKED AWAY,
IF YOU COULD LIVE THAT DAY OVER JUST WHAT WOULD YOU SAY?
I'LL BE YOUR MASTER, YOU'LL BE MY SLAVE,
I'LL EVEN GO WITH YOU WHEN YOU GO TO THE GRAVE.
NOW YOU HAVE MET ME, WHAT WILL YOU DO?
WILL YOU TRY ME OR NOT: IT'S ALL UP TO YOU.
I CAN BRING YOU MORE MISERY THAN WORDS CAN TELL,
COME TAKE MY HAND LET ME LEAD YOU TO HELL.

By Alicia Van Davis, a young woman who wrote this poem while she was in gaol for drug offences. When she was released, she remained true to her story; The drug owned her. She was found dead with a needle still in her arm.

The War on Drugs

Politicians usually focus on economic issues. It is therefore ironic that, when it comes to the illicit drug industry, most politicians choose to ignore the enormous amounts of money that are being wasted through policies which emphasise criminality and imprisonment.

Criminalisation only drives users and the illegal drug trade underground. It prevents the registration and control of lethal substances which are regularly consumed by people living with addictions. The illegal market is booming. Drug cartels around the world are making millions while, at the same time, most politicians shun scientific evidence and ignore the devastating impact the illicit drug trade is having on the communities that they are supposed to represent.

There is a flicker of light, giving hope that we are starting to penetrate the folly of the past. For example, in Holland, drugs are available in controlled environments. This is in no way a drug 'free for all' as there is widespread education to discourage drug use and warning of its consequences. Treatment and prevention are integrated, decreasing pressure on users to commit crimes such as armed robbery to fund their habits. This can only be a good thing.

In Holland, a distinction is drawn between 'hard' drugs (such as heroin), and the temporary use of so-called 'soft' drugs (such as cannabis). Access to controlled outlets for soft drugs decreases the risk of potential users being exposed to criminal street dealers.

The Dutch strategy has led to improved attitudes among police and other officials. Significantly, such approaches encourage law enforcement in ways that promote dignity, seeing vulnerable people rather than applying the labels of 'drug addict' and 'criminal' in the first instance. Dutch authorities differentiate between 'big dealers' and 'small users'.

Decriminalisation of drug use grants governments power to control supplies and stop profits going to criminal organisations.

Spiritual Dimension

Communism's most zealous intellectual, Karl Marx, pronounced in 1844 that religion is the 'opiate of the masses'. It could be said that illicit drug use is the 'religion' of those living with addiction.

There is certainly camaraderie among prisoners when they get a chance to drink a clandestine 'brew' or dabble in drugs.

In hearing the stories of prisoners, I have come to learn things I might otherwise not know. Certain protocols are observed. If prisoners are engaging in illicit consumption, they only take one drag of a 'spliff' being passed round or one swig out of the container of liquor. They never ask others in the group for drugs, but rather wait to be offered. As a group of prisoners partake, they 'mellow out' together. There is no past or future, only now. Some may argue that there is something of the spiritual in these experiences.

Entheogens are psychoactive substances known for their religious or spiritual effects. They have been used for thousands of years and include cannabis, ethanol, psilocybin mushrooms and opium.

A Different Space

Now in his 40s, Christopher has been in and out of prison for years for relatively minor offences. He has smoked cannabis for more than 25 years, a habit he attributes to 'a spiritual-mystical appreciation of its effects', which he describes as follows:

It takes me out of myself and my problems. I am in a different space, able to relax, chill out. The world feels different and I have more appreciation of nature. My ideal life would be to live in a small community in the country, away from all the shit that goes on here. Grow my own stuff to smoke and be left to live my life in peace with like-minded people.

When Christopher is in prison he regularly attends chapel services, Bible study groups and the like. He sees no contradiction between his use of cannabis and his Christian faith. Unlike Christopher, most drug-users would not directly interpret the effects of their drug use as entering into a religious or spiritual realm.

Bootlegging

Other prisoners are intent on 'setting up a brew' (a manufactured alcoholic drink). It tends to be made of fruit that has fermented and yeast if it can be obtained, plus anything else that might increase alcoholic content. Once the components are assembled, a place is found to hide it away until maturity. This may entail burying it with a concealed above-ground pipe outlet, or finding some other location where it is unlikely to be found. However, most of these illicit brews are discovered. Sometimes the game is up when prisoners are seen to be intoxicated. There are added dangers with this kind of alcoholic concoction. There is always uncertainty as to how the end product will turn out. The liquid can be poisonous and the alcoholic content lethal.

In Sickness and in Death

Lord God,
I give thanks for the medicinal drugs you have provided for us,
originally resourced from nature and the natural world.

Thank you for the knowledge you have given to researchers and medical professionals
...enabling lives to be saved through the use of drugs.
For I (and millions of other people) would be dead
without these developments in medicine.

But Lord!
Human beings have messed up!
In the prisons, drugs cause sickness and death
...instead of healing.
Most of the people in here have drug problems
...making   ...buying   ...selling   ...using
Slowly but surely it's killing them!

Yesterday I was talking to Owen,
who has been an addict of illegal drugs for years.
That's why he has spent
...more than half his life in prison.
Locking him up is no use.
He gets drugs in here almost as easily
as getting them out there.
He needs treatment rather than punishment.
So that he can get better, or at least learn to manage his addiction.

Lord,
This seems to be such an enormous and difficult problem,
there is nothing I can do, at the moment
...except pray.

I pray for Owen and the many others like him
who are locked into the illegal drugs trade.
I pray for the authorities, those making our laws,
that they may open their eyes and see things as they really are.

Oh God!
We need to see people living with addiction as needing medical care.
We must stop and provide support
rather than simply throwing them into prison.

MIND THE GAP

CHAPTER 4

VICTIMS & OFFENDERS

'They all look the same'

The prison dentist and his nurse assistant were white. Two black prisoners were waiting for treatment. One had a painkilling injection and was told to go back to the waiting room until it took effect. He went to the adjacent toilet, two minutes later the nurse assistant mistakenly led the other prisoner to the dentist's chair. 'Open up' said the dentist and pulled a tooth from his unanaesthetised mouth. His screams could be heard all over the prison. The nurse assistant said 'They [black prisoners] all look the same to me'.[1]

1 *How to Survive in the Nick*, Marshall J, 1974.

Train Timetables

A small group of prisoners was sitting with a chaplain, during a lunch break. One guy spoke up about his attempt to commit suicide:

I went and had a couple of beers then walked down the railway embankment and lay down across the railway lines. I was there for ages. Nothing happened, no trains. It was so hot. I thought: 'Bugger it. I'll go and have a couple more beers and then come back.' When I had a couple, I changed my mind and went home.

Another guy said, with a deadpan expression: 'Next time, you'd better check the train timetable first.'

Impact

Most prisoners spend very little, if any, time thinking about the impact of their crimes on victims.

Harry said:

I never really thought about the damage or the pain I was inflicting on the people closest to me. I was also blind to the fact that, through my criminal actions, violence, and general disregard for the people around me, I was devastating so many people—both directly and indirectly.

Who are the Victims?

Just about everyone who has a connection with victims and offenders is affected by crime. Severity of effects ranges from a range of physical, psychological and emotional losses to death. Tragically some victims suffer for the rest of their lives. Traumatic consequences for families can range from bereavement and deep sadness, to outrage and anger, even a desire to seek vengeance. Crime can create an atmosphere of fear, with us all worrying more about those who are near and dear to us. Some people experience a form of psychological paralysis, often diagnosed as Post-traumatic stress and complex post-traumatic stress disorders. Typically, in such circumstances, victims struggle with the shock of being violated for the remainder of their lives.

Blaming Substance Abuse

Offenders commonly attempt to diminish their own responsibility by blaming the influence of drugs and alcohol. I have often heard offenders say: 'When it happened, it was because of alcohol (or drugs)' or 'I was out of it, off my head. I'm not sure what happened. I can't remember.'

While such memory lapses are often genuine, they do not excuse offenders' responsibilities for their own actions. Unfortunately, a high proportion of criminals are pathological, manipulative and just downright liars. Instead of telling the whole truth, they only reveal details that portray them in a positive light. Some offenders are so used to tailoring the truth to their own advantage that they have lost the capacity to know how to be honest! From what I have seen, the vast majority of 'blame the drugs and alcohol' yarns that are spun in prison are nothing more than offenders seeking to escape responsibility and avoid the consequences of their actions.

Blaming the Victim

Gerry received a lengthy sentence for an armed robbery in which he pulled out a replica gun at a petrol station. He said:

I didn't hurt the bloke. I never intended to. There was no blood. It wasn't a real gun. The bloke overreacted.

Gerry's victim was so frightened that he collapsed with a suspected heart attack but Gerry did not understand what all the fuss was about. He could not see how shoving a gun into a man's face could be so traumatic that the victim might never fully recover.

Murky Circumstances

George complained bitterly, over a number of years, that it was unfair that he had received a life sentence for murder. His violent act had taken place in the murky circumstances of George and his victim drinking alcohol and injecting drugs. George swore that he had only picked up a kitchen knife in self-defence. However, when evidence was heard in court, the jury rejected his plea of self-defence. He was convicted of murder.

Nick, who was serving a lengthy term for grievous bodily harm against his female partner, also railed against his sentence. He protested:

Last time I was in prison, I found out the slag was shagging another bloke! So, I gave her 'a belting' when I got out. It was her fault, not mine.

Nick's partner, ended up in hospital with broken ribs, lacerations and concussion. As a prisoner who had been 'in' and 'out' for years, he had no comprehension of the struggles that his partner faced when he was inside. He did not want to know about her loneliness, frustration and debt.

This poor woman told me how she had lived hand-to-mouth, week after week, trying to bring up three boys so that they did not follow in Nick's footsteps. I dip my hat to her. I think it is truly remarkable that she stuck with Nick as long as she did. Sadly, this determination and stamina cost her dearly.

Carl was on remand in prison and facing charges of sexual assault. He was indignant:

'She gave me the "come on", stuck her boobs in my face. She had this mini skirt on. She was asking for it.'

Severely Beaten

Zara was born in Britain after her parents and extended family arrived from the Indian sub-continent. Culturally, they were conservative and traditional, especially when it came to boy-girl relationships. Zara was expected to conform, and respect her parents' choice of husband for her. (This would probably be someone in Pakistan whom she had never seen.)

When, as a 16-year-old, she expressed reservations about these plans, she was beaten and locked in her room. This went on for several days until an older brother unlocked her door to get her out of the house. She ended up in a women's domestic violence refuge.

When Zara's family found her, she received a severe beating. Eventually, two men and a woman were convicted of causing her grievous bodily harm. In conversation with me, one of these men expressed no remorse. He maintained that Zara, having offended against her family's honour, was lucky to escape with her life. He considered himself to be the victim and blamed her for his plight.

Trapped in Unfortunate Circumstances

It is so tragic to see many young people from poorer communities often with little education and virtually no life aspirations. They do not even know what day it is, because every day seems the same. While a difficult socio-economic background is no excuse for criminal behaviour, it does place it in context.

Colin came from a poverty-stricken housing estate on the edge of a large city. The manufacturing industries that had employed most of the people living on the estate had closed due to an economic downturn. Colin had left school early and had no academic qualifications. He was barely literate. As I got to know him, he started to tell me about his life. He said:

I started nicking cars when I was 16. I like driving. I couldn't buy a car, never had no job, no money. I thought, if they can have a car I'll take one of theirs. I only took posh cars off posh people who were loaded. We used to take the cars down the park and do wheelies on the grass. Sometimes, we would take a stretch of road and have time trials on it, see who could get from one end to the other the quickest. Then, we used to go on the motorway and see how fast we could go. We'd dump the car somewhere not too far from home, if the coppers didn't get us first. It was cool.

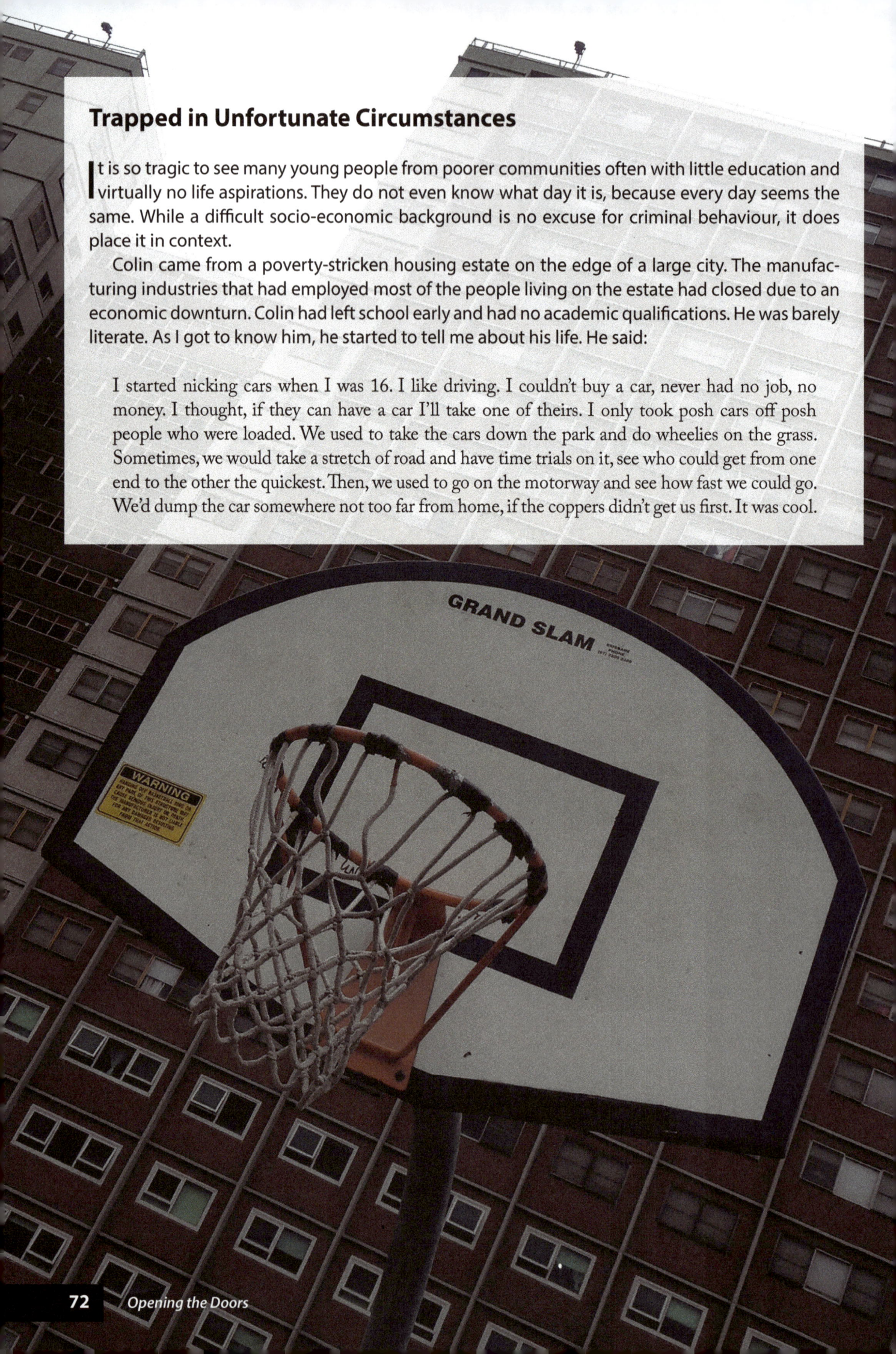

Life Sentence

Janice was serving a life sentence for murdering her husband. She claimed that he had 'knocked her about' physically and sexually for years. She said:

I got to the end of my tether. I couldn't take any more from that bastard. He came home pissed as usual. He hit me and forced me to have sex with him. When he was sleeping, I hit him over the head with a hammer and killed him.

The jury rejected Janice's claim of provocation. She is now serving a life sentence for murder.

Keep Dealing

Ivan had been in and out of prison, and involved in the illegal drug trade, for years. He blamed his recidivist track record on debts to drug dealers. His latest sentence for trafficking was substantial. He maintained that he wanted to get clean and out of the trade for good. He explained:

> But I can't. I've got drug debts. The only way I can pay them is to keep dealing or the bastards will do me over. Even in here, I can't get away from them.

A Perpetrator's Family

Lord,
I went to see the parents of a teenager who is on remand,
after being arrested and charged,
over a particularly horrific murder.

When I knocked on the door,
they were reluctant to let me into the house.
They are being pestered day and night by the media,
as well as receiving toxic phone calls and mail.

I have seen them coming to the prison for visits.
They are distressed and heartbroken about what's happened.
They told me they can't stay in their present neighbourhood,
…where they have lived since their two sons were born.
They are planning to move as soon as possible.

Lord,
I promised that I (and others)
would do what we can to support their boy.
We'll do our best to keep him out of harm's way.
I left my contact details.
Lord, I think my visit probably helped a bit.
I hope so.
It's not going to be easy for them, far from it.

One Night of Foolishness

Basil was arrested and imprisoned prior to a successful application for bail. He was in his 40s, a seemingly respectable citizen with a settled marriage, three teenage children and a middle-management job.

One night, he had too much to drink and risked driving home. He drifted into oncoming traffic and hit a vehicle carrying an eleven-year-old boy and his mother. The boy was killed. The woman escaped with relatively minor physical injuries.

The implications for the family of the dead boy were enormous, as they were for Basil's family when he subsequently received a term of imprisonment. He lost his job. The mortgage could not be paid and the family had to move into rented accommodation. His teenage children were mortified at the media publicity about their father, which was unforgiving.

All involved became victims as a result of Basil's one night of foolishness.

A 'Deal'

I got to know Rob over several years. One day he told me his story.

Rob said that before he came to prison he had been an active member of a criminal gang in New South Wales which was involved in 'pimping' prostitutes, drug trafficking, robbery, fraud and 'protection' rackets. He said that, when police were closing in on the gang's activities, they needed evidence from a gang member to get convictions. Rob was offered a 'deal'.

In exchange for giving evidence, he was promised a sentence considerably shorter than other gang members. He was also offered the chance to serve his sentence in a prison on the other side of the country and be given a new identity so he can never be traced. Rob cooperated with his prosecutors rather spend the rest of his life in prison.

After the trials he simply 'disappeared'.

Annie and her Children

Lord,
I visited Annie at home today.
Last week her partner got four years for drug
    offences.
It's the umpteenth time he's been in prison.
She is sick to death of it and is barely coping.
She has to deal with everything
…kids
…bills
…debts
…rent
She and her kids are victims of his criminal
    stupidity!

Annie tells me that her 14-year-old daughter is
    having sex with an older bloke.
The only thing Annie can do is get the girl 'on
    the pill'
…but she doesn't take it unless nagged by her
    Mum.
A teenage pregnancy would be the final straw!

Joe, the partner and father, raves on about what
    he'll do
…to the bloke
…when he gets out.
If he was at all responsible
…this wouldn't be happening!

Lord,
I want to get Annie a financial counsellor
…to negotiate essentials like rent, gas and
    electricity.
And also food.
But Lord!
This is all Band-Aid stuff,
rather than a real solution.
There are hundreds of families in the same boat.
I see some of them every day!
We do what we can.
But it's not enough!

Lord:
I really have fears about the potential for
    murder-suicide,
with some of these families.
The partner on the outside,
battling to keep things going.
It all gets too much…
Mum kills the kids,
and then herself.

Lord,
As far as I can tell,
Annie is not at that point
…yet!
But, I pray for her, the kids, and other families;
those who might be tempted to opt for that
    solution.

Scum Visiting Scum

I got to know Sarah and her children when she came to visit her partner in prison. He had been in and out of prison for years. She was a lonely person with very little support. One day she said:

> Sometimes I feel like scum visiting scum. It depends who's on duty at the gate and who's doing the security checks. Some of the officers are kind to us. Others seem to go out of their way to piss us about.

Sarah had three children between the ages of three and eleven to look after while their dad was locked-up. He bullied her to visit, with the kids, and made veiled threats about what would happen if she refused. Their home, privately rented from an exploitative landlord, was one and half hour's travelling time away from the prison, if they travelled on public transport.

By the time Sarah got to the prison she described herself as 'knackered', especially if the kids were playing up. Consequently, her one hour visit could be a tense affair. She told me that, when she got home after her visits, all she could do was 'stick the kids in front of the telly with a bag of chips.' She said that, when her partner rang from prison to check up on them, she wanted to 'tell him to fuck off.'

So I wondered: 'Why did she stick with him?' She reflected:

> I love him, I think. I did once. Every time he goes inside, he swears blind this will be the last stretch, but it never is. I'm frightened of him. If I tried to end our relationship, he'd find me and the kids when he came out, or send someone round while he's still inside. I don't know what to do.

Never Got Over It

Jenny was running a corner shop which was open 12 hours a day. She had to compete with supermarkets to make a living. One evening, shortly before closing time, a bloke came into the shop wearing a balaclava. He waved a gun and demanded the contents of the till. Five years later, Jenny spoke of her experience:

> I've never got over it. I thought I was going to die when he pointed the gun in my face and started swearing and screaming at me. I managed to open the till, and then I froze. He grabbed the money and ran. I couldn't carry on with the business after that. I had nightmares. I was nervous it might happen again. I got some pills to calm me down but it was no good. I'm still nervous after all this time.

Jenny's husband Ted, said:

> She worries about the bastard coming out of prison. I'll kill him if he ever comes near here.

A Few Hours Before ...

Stewart and his wider family became secondary victims following a tragic series of events. His 18-year-old son was killed in a road accident while riding his motor bike. The driver of the car was charged with causing death by dangerous driving. Stewart was sitting in court when one of his daughters was called as a witness.

As the evidence unfolded, Stewart heard something that totally shocked him. The daughter said that her brother had smoked cannabis a few hours before riding the motor bike. This was also confirmed by pathology. Evidence was given that the cannabis levels in the deceased rider may have impaired his judgement.

On top of losing their son, Stewart and his partner had to face evidence of their son's drug use. Court proceedings can throw up all sorts of unexpected negative issues for secondary victims, which add to the trauma.

Our Nightmare Had Begun

Karen's daughter Jess was 15 when she was murdered. She said:

Jess met a boy who was a disc jockey. He had recently broken up his relationship with another girl who was a bit older than Jess. I was overseas on holiday and received a phone call. I was told that Jess had been murdered, stabbed to death, in our home. Later, I found out that the person who murdered our daughter was the girl that used to go out with the boy Jess had met. The girl was jealous. She came to our home with a knife and stabbed Jess 47 times. She died on the kitchen floor. Her dad came home from work and found her there. Our nightmare had begun.

It is hard to describe what the next few years were like, trying to pick up the pieces after such a horrific event—I don't know how we survived. Secondary victims like us become prisoners too, trapped in pain, fear and sometimes hate. Some of Jess's friends couldn't cope. The world, as they knew it, had turned on its head. Things didn't make sense anymore. Several of Jess's friends went severely off the rails.[1]

---

1   *Shafts of Light from a Dark Place: The Story of the Sycamore Tree Project 2005–2008 as told by the Participants* (Perth: Prison Fellowship, 2008), 8–9.

A Blessed Relief

Lord,
Danny is up on a charge of murder.
He has been abandoned by friends and family.
He has no-one to support him in court
…except his lawyer
…and You Lord.
That's why I'm attending.

Lord,
I go down to the cells to see him during the lunch break.
He seems to think he is going to be convicted.
He is probably right.

Perhaps he should change his plea to guilty?
It would give the victim's family some respite
…from listening to all the horrible details.

Lord,
He is afraid of the consequences.
if he's found guilty.
But it might be a blessed relief
…for him
…and everyone else.
Apparently it's no surprise to people who have known him in the past,
that he's up on a murder charge.

Lord,
From what he has told me,
violence has been a 'normal' part of life
…ever since he was a child
…having to steal
…fight to eat
…survive.

My heart bleeds for the family of the deceased.
It must be devastating to have to listen, to all the gruesome details,
especially for his parents and sister.
As long as they live,
they will never recover from the trauma of losing their son and brother,
in such a violent way.

They don't seem angry
…but traumatised
…bewildered.
Lord, I pray for them.
Somehow this family needs to be supported.

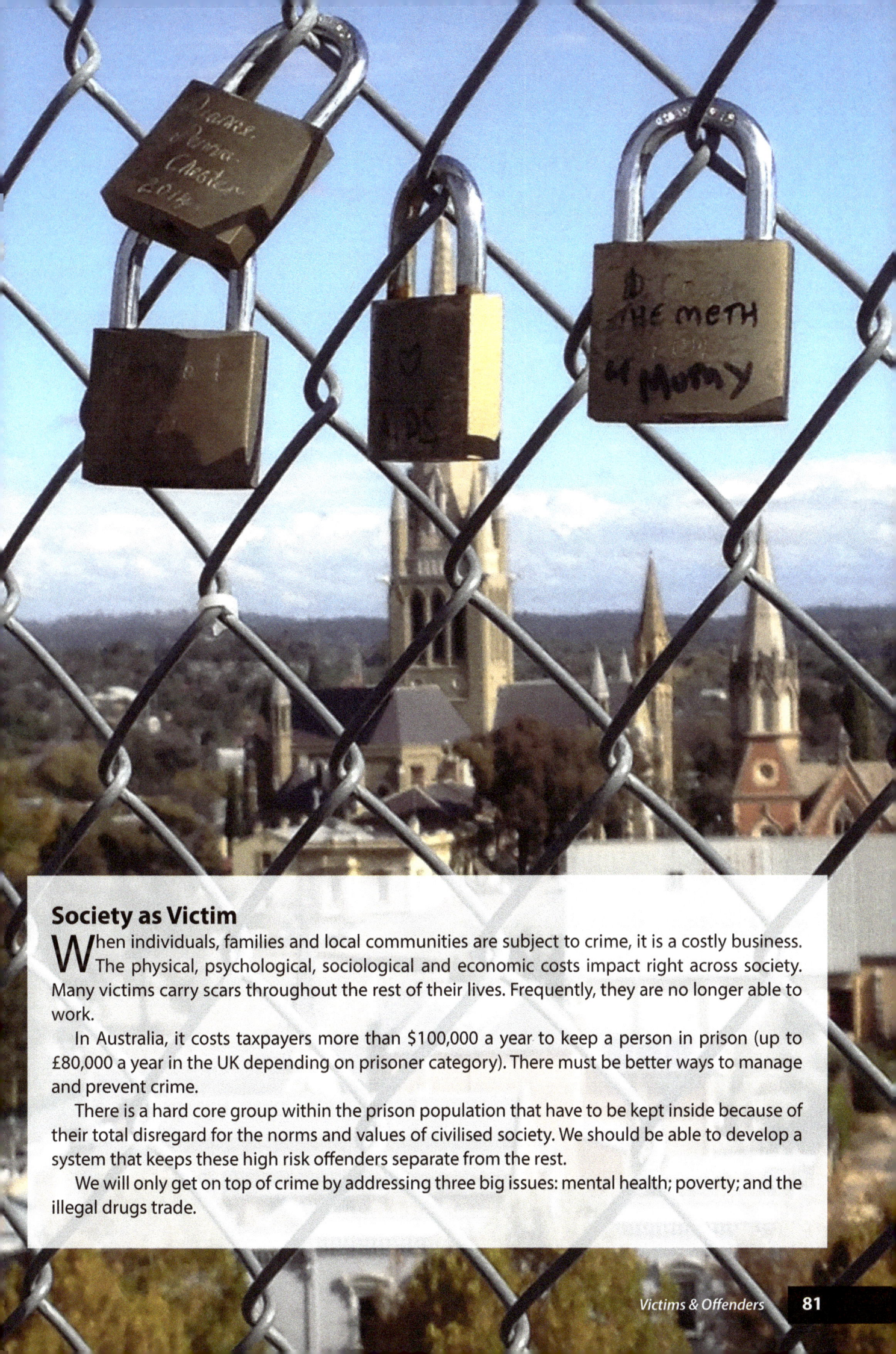

Society as Victim

When individuals, families and local communities are subject to crime, it is a costly business. The physical, psychological, sociological and economic costs impact right across society. Many victims carry scars throughout the rest of their lives. Frequently, they are no longer able to work.

In Australia, it costs taxpayers more than $100,000 a year to keep a person in prison (up to £80,000 a year in the UK depending on prisoner category). There must be better ways to manage and prevent crime.

There is a hard core group within the prison population that have to be kept inside because of their total disregard for the norms and values of civilised society. We should be able to develop a system that keeps these high risk offenders separate from the rest.

We will only get on top of crime by addressing three big issues: mental health; poverty; and the illegal drugs trade.

Witnesses

It can be very traumatic to be a victim of crime or a prosecution witness. Courtroom cross-examination often requires witnesses to relive their experiences over and over, sometimes confined to the witness box for days on end.

In the Same Room

Damien's house was broken into and when he confronted the trespasser he was badly beaten. He spent a long time in hospital. His physical injuries were so severe that he will never fully recover. Similarly, his psychological equilibrium was damaged. His assailant was remanded in custody until he was brought to trial some months later. Damien dreaded the thought of being in the same courtroom as the accused. He said: 'When I saw him I started to physically shake. I couldn't breathe properly. It was a nightmare.'

The court was adjourned and provision was made for Damien to give evidence from a separate room via video link.

Closing Our Doors

Ellie, 19, and her older sister Pippa, ran a boutique. One evening, as they were about to close, two guys came in. One pointed a gun at them and demanded the contents of the till, their mobile phones and a gold bracelet. A similar thing happened several weeks later.

'It gave me nightmares,' Pippa said. 'I was too scared to come to work.' The two sisters are still shaken. 'We've started closing our doors when it gets dark, and I jump to conclusions about customers that come in,' Pippa said. 'It's nerve-wracking.'

It turned out that these crimes were two of a string of hold-ups which occurred over several months. The probability is that the sisters will not be required to give evidence in court because the offenders were clearly identified by Closed Circuit Television footage.

Many witnesses are reluctant to give evidence because they think it could put them, or their loved ones, at risk of revenge attacks from the offenders or their associates.

Looking after Us?

The partner of a prisoner said:

> The police want me to give evidence against my 'ex' and others who are involved in a drugs racket. The punters and dealers used to come here at all hours of the day or night. If I grass them up, they will kill me, and what about the kids? He is not their father. He doesn't give a shit about me or them. The police say they will look after us, find us another place to live. How can they? I don't trust them. All they are interested in is getting convictions. They don't give a shit about me and the kids. I could lose custody of them if I get involved. I can't let that happen.

Going Public

Peter was in a bar frequented primarily by gay men. Four men in the bar got involved in a dispute which led to a fight. One of the participants was badly hurt. Unfortunately, the guy who was arrested and charged was not actually the main offender. When the case came to trial, Peter was asked to be a witness for the defence. Until that time, he had kept his sexual orientation a secret from his family. He feared that, if he gave evidence, his whereabouts on the evening of the incident would be made public.

Storybook Dads

Each year in the United Kingdom, about 160,000 children experience the trauma of a parent going to prison. Support for these children is limited. They often experience feelings of abandonment, isolation and shame. This can lead to low self-esteem, poor performance at school, delinquency and intergenerational offending. Prisoners' children are three times more likely to suffer from mental health issues.

Storybook Dads is a charity that began at Dartmoor Prison in 2003 and now operates in numerous prisons. Imprisoned parents maintain family ties by reading bedtime stories for their children. Provision is made for poor readers and non-readers to participate by reading the story line by line after a good reader. The stories are recorded and edited in the prisons. Music and sound effects are added to make the stories come alive. Then, the finished CD is sent to the child.

A nine-year-old girl said: 'I worry about my dad in prison, but he sounds happy on the CD and that makes me feel happy too.'

A seven-year-old said: 'I miss my dad so much. When I feel lonely, I listen to my CD and hearing his voice makes me feel better.'

A prisoner said: 'My son is autistic so it's hard to talk on the phone. He listens to his CD so much he's nearly worn it out.'

Prisoners who keep in touch with their children are less likely to reoffend upon release. Feedback from prisoners shows that 96 percent of those taking part in Storybook Dads read to their children regularly when they are released.

Support Services for Victims and Witnesses

Victims and witnesses have the right to be treated with dignity compassion and respect, particularly in relation to their cultural and religious backgrounds.

They are entitled to information about support services including medical, counselling and legal help. They should be kept informed as investigations and prosecution proceed. Whilst the case is in court, victims and witnesses are provided with protection from contact with the accused person and defence witnesses.

Victims also have the right to make 'victim impact statements', outlining to the court how the crime has affected them. Help is available to prepare this, if required.

Victims and witnesses will be informed when the offender applies for parole, is to be released, or escapes from gaol.

In Australia, victims have the right to apply for compensation through the Victims of Crime Assistance Tribunal (or in England the Criminal Injuries Compensation Authority).

In many countries, including Australia, England and Wales, the Victim Support network provides simple but comprehensive information about crime, its impact, sources of support and advice. The organisation's community directory includes women's refuges, victim support agencies, financial assistance and homicide support groups.

A mother said:

My daughter was raped last year. If it wasn't for Victim Support, I don't know how we would have survived. We were believed. That means a lot to me. Victim Support has been there for us, for the medicals at the hospital, throughout court and so on. My support worker has helped me through the tears and anger. All the help has made us stronger. We know help is only a phone call away. This is the biggest thing we have had to face. Victim Support sticks by you. We are very thankful to them.

Victim Support Agencies

These are a selection of support services in the UK. There are similar services in many countries.

- Criminal Injuries Compensation Authority
  www.gov.uk/government/organisations/
  criminal-injuries-compensation-authority
- National Association for People Abused in Childhood: www.napac.org.uk
- National Stalking Helpline: www.stalkinghelpline.org
- Rape Crisis England and Wales: www.rapecrisis.org.uk
- Support after Murder and Manslaughter: www.samm.org.uk
- Support Line: www.supportline.org.uk
- Victims' Information Service: www.victimsinformationservice.org.uk
- Victim Support: www.victimsupport.org.uk

CHAPTER 5

JUSTICE?

Only Trying to Help

A prisoner was walking from death row to the gas chamber accompanied by the prison chaplain. The chaplain said: 'Once the gas comes through, take a deep breath and it won't hurt so much.' The condemned man replied: 'How the hell do you know?'

Justice can be hard to attain, especially if you are poor. Legal fees are now out of reach of ordinary people. Similarly, those who have limited access to money, find it difficult to obtain legal representation if they get into trouble with the law.

Sadly, Government-funded 'duty lawyers' often do not have the time to properly prepare for cases. I have met many people in prison who were indignant about the poor legal representation that they received in court. For some people, the time afforded to them by court-appointed lawyers was as little as five minutes before the start of a hearing. In some cases this can lead to miscarriages of justice.

Punitive Justice

Historically, prisons were places where punishment and suffering were to be inflicted on criminals, so as to diminish the likelihood of repeat offending and act as a deterrent within the wider community.

A Chief Justice of England in 1859–1880 summed up this type of justice: 'The prime objective [of imprisonment] is to deter through suffering inflicted as a punishment for crime, and the fear of a repetition of it. If, as a by-product, the reformation of the offender is achieved so much the better. If not, no matter. It is hardly to be expected.'[1]

In many towns, villages and cities throughout the UK, it is still possible to see what remains of an ancient form of punishment known as 'the stocks'. Offenders would be apprehended, publicly paraded through the streets, before being locked into these torturous contraptions and subjected to abuse and ridicule. Up until the middle of the 19th century, public hangings were also the norm. Such shaming techniques and brutality were intended to deter others from criminal activity.

Approaches to justice which seek to prioritise punishment can be simply knee-jerk reactions to crime and its impact upon innocent victims. As a result such strategies risk being superficial; not actually addressing the pain of victims, rehabilitating offenders, or lessening the impact of crime on the wider community. Indeed, brutal prison environments which dehumanise and humiliate offenders are more likely to provoke anger and resentment, thus increasing crime and violence.

---

1 Poster at Dartmoor Prison Museum, viewed 2013.

Treasure in the Heart of Every Man

The mood and temper of the public in regard to the treatment of crime and criminals is one of the most unfailing tests of the civilisation of a country. There needs to be constant heart searching by all charged with the duty of punishment, a desire and eagerness to rehabilitate all who have paid their dues in the hard coinage of punishment, tireless efforts towards the discovery of curative and regenerating processes, and an unfaltering faith that there is a treasure in the heart of very man if you can only find it.[1]

1   Winston Churchill addressing the House of Commons, as Home Secretary, recorded in *Hansard* (London), 20 July 1910. No doubt this arose out of the heart of a politician who was reflecting on his own experience as a prisoner-of-war in South Africa during the Boer War.

Rehabilitative Justice

Approaches which emphasise rehabilitation and treatment for offenders are more forward-thinking and pragmatic, making allowances for sociological inequalities which contribute to crime. While rehabilitative justice does not deny that offenders have personal responsibilities when choosing to act illegally, it accepts that socio-economic disadvantage and psychological pressure can increase the likelihood of some people overstepping legal boundaries. Such risk factors might include substance addiction, mental health issues, homelessness, unemployment and lack of education.

The main criticism of rehabilitative justice is that it focuses almost exclusively on the needs of the criminals, aiming to reduce repeat offences by addressing the factors that have contributed to their social and personal disadvantage. In this framework of justice, only minimal attention is given to the needs of victims. There is no attempt to confront offenders with the seriousness of their behaviour and implications for victims.

For rehabilitation to be truly effective, it must include opportunities for victims to communicate the impact of crime on their lives, and perpetrators to take responsibility for damage caused and opportunities for restitution where possible.

Restorative Justice

Restorative justice has been described as 'addressing the hurts and needs of the victims, and the hurts and needs of the offenders, in such a way that they and the community might be healed.'

In processes of restorative justice, offenders are asked to admit their crimes and acknowledge the impact these have had on victims, their families and the wider community. Offenders are asked to apologise, make reparation and do whatever is possible to right the wrong they have caused.

Ideally, three parties are represented in processes of restorative justice: offenders, victims and representatives of the communities in which the crimes occurred.

An issue with this model of justice is that it is usually premised on conversations occurring between criminals and victims, or their representatives. While some victims and their families find that such conversations contribute to their sense of resolution and healing, others would find them retraumatising and a risk to emotional, psychological and even physical safety. In many cases, it is difficult for victims to see their perpetrator, even via video screen, let alone engage in face-to-face conversation.

I Wish I Had Been Killed ...

John and Greg were best mates. They went out one evening, had a few drinks and smoked cannabis. They stole a car and went for a 'burn' around some country roads. John, who was driving, ignored a warning sign to slow down as they approached a bend. The car flipped over. Greg was killed. John received minor injuries.

John was charged and convicted of car theft, causing death by dangerous driving, driving without a licence, driving while over the alcohol limit and while affected by illegal substances. He was banned from driving and received a substantial term of imprisonment. When delivering the sentence the judge remarked that John had 'shown no remorse'.

Greg's family were satisfied with the outcome of the trial, but devastated by the events leading up to it. About six months later, his sister Lyn got in touch with prison authorities, saying that she would like to see John to ask 'Why?' and 'How come he didn't show any remorse?'

A restorative justice meeting was facilitated by a social worker. Along with John and Lyn, a prison officer and chaplain were also in attendance.

As soon as Lyn entered the room, John said: 'I'm sorry.'

Lyn responded: 'You didn't seem sorry at the time and during the trial.' He replied:

> I was playing tough. I knew I would be coming back here and I didn't want this lot in here to think I was weak. You know Greg was my best mate. I have been upset and sorry ever since. I feel it every day and would give anything to have him back and that time over again. Sometimes, I wish I had been killed instead of him, or as well as. We were so stupid, but it's too late. I can't do anything. I wanted to send some flowers to the funeral but wasn't allowed. I don't know where he is buried but when I get out I would like to put some flowers on his grave, if the family don't mind.

After the meeting Lyn said:

> I feel better about things now. It was a crazy accident. I can see he's sorry. He was upset and I don't think he was putting it on. Greg and him were quite close and spent a fair bit of time together. I am going home to talk to Mum and Dad and the others. They didn't really want me to come but I am glad I did and I think, when I tell them how he was and what he said, it will help them to stop feeling angry. I hope so anyway. These last months have been really hard for us, especially Mum and Dad. I will probably visit John again. The prison is going to let him get some flowers for Greg. So I will take them to the cemetery.

Violated and Traumatised

A victim of sexual assault said:

I am not 100 percent over it. Mainly it's fear. Fear of the dark, fear of strangers. I can't get it under control. It is always there. Now, I don't walk to and from work. My boyfriend always meets me. I will never get back to being the same as I was before the attack. I hope I can learn to live with it.

A bank teller described the trauma he experienced in response to a robbery:

At first I was startled and then the reality hit me. I was completely under the control of the robbers. They had the power to do whatever they wanted. I went numb. It was only afterwards that I felt sick. For years after, I felt a miserable combination of fear and anger, whenever I was startled by an unfamiliar sound or someone raised their voice at work, I would break out in a sweat.

Community Responses

We need to rediscover ways to deal with conflict and resolve justice issues. This requires us to think seriously about our community's values and to commit to dealing with wrongdoing when these are violated.

Indigenous communities have practised their own forms of community-based justice for millennia.

While western societies have long focussed on punishing and reforming criminals, we face major difficulties when it comes to safely reintegrating criminals back into communities.

Information gained through restorative justice processes, particularly face-to-face conversations with criminals, can help to address social problems and make communities safer. Social planners need to seriously consider whether crimes were premeditated or occurred at random. They also need to compare the rates of violence in family situations with the targeting of strangers, and assess whether security improvements, such as lighting and 'safe house' campaigns would make a difference. Also they need to analyse the extent to which poverty, desperation, alcohol and drug addiction, revenge and discrimination contribute to crimes in their local areas.

A 'Crack Head' Learns to Read and Write

Two young women who had experienced a burglary requested a restorative justice conference with the offender who was serving a prison sentence. The offender agreed to this, and a psychologist chaired the meeting.

The women described how the burglary had affected them, particularly how upset they were at the invasion of their private space, the mess that had been left behind and, worst of all, their anxiety that it would happen again.

The offender explained his upbringing as background information, rather than offering it as an excuse. His mother was 15 when he was born and she had no capacity to look after him. His childhood was disrupted as he was shunted between different foster parents and institutional care. He had little education and was almost illiterate, having been excluded from school for fighting. Eventually, he joined a gang. He started drinking and taking drugs. He said he was a 'crack head' who lived mostly in squats, night shelters and on the streets.

The psychologist asked what the burglar could do to make restitution to his victims and get help for his future. They all agreed that he should attend literacy classes and a Narcotics Anonymous group within the prison, as well as seeking medical treatment for his addictions. The women asked that the offender write to them once a month to report how he was progressing. Initially, he needed to dictate his letters because he could not read and write. The women indicated their strong desire to visit for further conversation.

The Sycamore Tree Project

The Sycamore Tree Project has been running in prisons in many different countries for more than 20 years. It is based on a biblical story where Jesus gave Zacchaeus, a cheating tax collector, a chance to reform and be reintegrated into his community (Luke 19:1–10).

Seeking to offer contemporary prisoners new perspectives and opportunities to change their behaviour, the Sycamore Tree Project also emphasises the principle: '… In everything do to others as you would have them do to you.' (Matthew 7:12)

In the Zacchaeus story, Jesus entered the town of Jericho where word had got around that he was a great teacher and preacher. So, a crowd had gathered to hear what he had to say.

Zacchaeus, being rather short in stature, could not see Jesus. So, he ran ahead along the main road and climbed up into a sycamore tree. He now had a grandstand view and was able to hear some of the conversations between Jesus and others in the crowd.

Zacchaeus was a villain and a collaborator. He collected taxes from Jewish people for the hated Roman occupiers. Tax collectors were hated in that community but no-one dared to resist them because they were protected by the oppressive Romans.

As things turned out, when Jesus got to the sycamore tree he stopped, looked up, and called: 'Zacchaeus, hurry and come down; for I must stay at your house today.' (Luke 19:5). Zacchaeus was astonished but climbed out of the tree. He took Jesus home for a meal and provided him with a bed for the night. No doubt, Zacchaeus and Jesus talked over dinner and into the evening. This encounter changed Zacchaeus life. It resulted in him having a new perspective on life which affected everything he did. He exclaimed:

Look, half of my possessions, Lord, I will give to the poor; and if I have defrauded anyone of anything, I will pay back four times as much. (Luke 19:8)

The Sycamore Tree Project is offered to groups of six to ten prisoners. Also joining the group is a similar number of victims of crime. Victims are never placed in groups with their own perpetrators. Sessions have to be carefully organised to ensure that all activities conform to prison regulations. A member of the chaplaincy team usually gets this job. A facilitator from outside the prison is engaged to guide the group's discussions. The course is usually oversubscribed and waiting lists are common.

Some prisoners request admission to the Sycamore Tree Project, others are invited. When prisoners are asked why they want to participate, they usually say that other prisoners highly recommend the course.

A variety of issues are addressed in group discussions. In the first session, prisoners are asked to take responsibility for their offending behaviour. There are to be no excuses such as addiction or homelessness and no blaming victims or others. In a session on confession, prisoners are invited to tell the truth about their crimes. The next issue to be considered is the need for repentance, and a commitment to change. Subsequent sessions address issues such as forgiveness, reconciliation and making amends. For most offenders this is the first time that they have thought about how their actions impacted on victims. Consideration is given to whether a letter of apology, or offering some form of compensation, might be appropriate.

Each session may last for up to six hours, broken up with regular 'smoko' breaks and lunch. The group normally sits in a single circle, with prisoners and crime survivors intermingled. The facilitator sets guidelines for group discussions, confidentiality and safety. During each session, there will be an opportunity for one prisoner and one survivor to share their stories if they wish. There will be time for supportive comments and questions.

It is electrifying to hear people share their stories, often for the first time. Emotions are very intense and can sometimes spill over.

What Prisoners are Saying about the Sycamore Tree Project

'The Sycamore Tree Project changed my thinking. It's the first time I've ever done anything behind bars that has made me think about the crime I have done. It's made me stop and think, as I sat in my cell at night time, about what I've actually done and how it has affected people.'

'I have spent 13.5 of the last 15 years in prison. I have done countless courses—some good, some bad. Without a shadow of a doubt, the Sycamore Tree Project is the best thing that could ever have happened to me. The sheer rawness of emotion it delivers, the understanding and compassion it releases in people gives you a sense of hope for the future for everyone involved.'

'Prisoners need to be involved with what they have damaged, whether through work, education or other means. We are too far removed from the reality of our actions. Punishment is only a small part of rehabilitation and courses such as the Sycamore Tree Project go a long way to connecting the offender to his role in the suffering he has caused.'

'I have done ten years of an 18 year sentence for murder and I am now ready for this programme. For the first time, it is helping me to get to grips with what I did and why I did it. It is starting to give me some understanding of what my victim went through and what his family have been going through over all these years.'

Crime Survivors

The Sycamore Tree Project has also had a significant impact on the lives of crime survivors who have participated.

Melissa was a teller in a bank that was robbed. The offender pointed a gun at her. She took a month off work. Initially, she suffered from lack of sleep and a feeling that she wasn't safe anymore. A couple of years later, she participated as a crime survivor in a Sycamore Tree group in a prison. This helped her come to a point where she began to experience a form of forgiveness toward the person who offended against her. She said: 'I started to forgive him, so I could be set free.' Melissa is one crime survivor who is finding her own voice as she attempts to hold offenders accountable for what they have done.

Christine had never recovered from being the victim of a crime that had happened more than 25 years ago. She persistently felt unsafe. While participating in the Sycamore Tree Project, she was able to share her experience of being violated. She said that she felt as if she had experienced justice within the group as offenders took symbolic responsibility for the impact that the crime had on her life.

A secondary victim of a hideous crime who has participated in several Sycamore Tree Projects said:

In so many ways, secondary victims of crime are prisoners too—trapped in pain, fear, and sometimes hate. I wanted to be involved in the Sycamore Tree Project because I wanted to make something positive out of something so destructive. Working with offenders was a unique experience for me and it offered a chance for me to share my pain and bring home to them the reality of how violent crime impacts on families and communities.

For more information, see Prison Fellowship, *Shafts of Light from a Dark Place: The Story of the Sycamore Tree Project 2005–2008* (Perth: Prison Fellowship, 2008).

Ready for Change

Approaches to justice which emphasise punishment and revenge, fail to address the suffering of victims and do nothing to decrease the likelihood of repeat offences.

Rehabilitative justice provides treatment to offenders and attempts to address sociological disadvantages which contributed to them committing crimes. However, recognition of victims needs remains minimal. As one prisoner said:

Hearing stories from victims' perspectives can't not affect you. It was like someone had flicked a switch in my head. I am speaking to you in my victim's honour. I have made some mistakes but I am ready to change.

INDIGENOUS PRISONERS

Indigenous Prisoners

Colonisation by European Nations in North and South America, Africa, Asia and Australasia has robbed indigenous people of their culture and identity. They were viewed as pagans who needed converting to Christianity and primitive people who needed to be educated in the ways of Western society.

In almost every instance the colonists inflicted on indigenous people the principle of *Terra Nullius*, which can be translated as 'land of no people'. In practice this meant the colonists took, by force if necessary, land that had been sacred and tribal for many generations. Inevitably this led to conflict and the defeat and degradation of indigenous peoples who militarily were no match for the invaders.

Subsequent generations of indigenous people lost their culture and identity, and, with some notable exceptions, their dignity. They became the flotsam and jetsam on the margins of society, subject to persecution, abuse, and discrimination. Thankfully there are some signs of change in the 21st century but there is a long way to go before they regain their rightful place in mainstream societies.

Chapter 6 is one account of colonisation, in Australia, and the dire consequences for the indigenous people. Not least the fact that today in Western Australia they make up less than 3 percent of the general population and approximately 47 percent of the prison population.

Genocide

European colonists intentionally implemented policies of genocide in a bid to wipe out Australia's indigenous populations. Shamefully it was not until 1948, in the aftermath of the Holocaust, that the United Nations approved its 'Convention on the Prevention and Punishment of the Crime of Genocide'.

Tactics of genocide used in Australia include: killing Aborigines; imposing measures which prevented births within indigenous populations; and forcibly removing children from aboriginal families.

The European mindset of *Terra Nullius*, with its arrogant refusal to treat Aborigines as human, contributed to their annihilation.

In the 1950s, an Aboriginal man in his 80s told a story, remembered from his childhood, of how white men on horseback hunted indigenous people 'like animals'. When word got out that a hunting party of white settlers were on the move, his parents were hidden by his grandparents in thick scrub that was impenetrable on horseback.

Another aspect of genocide is the removal of indigenous and mixed race children from their families by compulsion, duress, trickery and subterfuge. The church and other social welfare institutions were complicit in this policy. Prior to 1911, and then under the Aboriginal Ordinance 1911, the Commonwealth Government gave the 'Chief Protector' and some of his staff, the power to act as the legal guardian of every Aborigine and person of mixed descent in the Northern Territory and the Australian Capital Territory until the age of 18. Similar arrangements were put in place in the other five states by State Governments. As a result of these policies, children were forcibly removed from their families and placed into government and church institutions across the country.

Such policies continued until the 1960s. Indigenous children were separated from their families and culture, and assimilated into institutions, under the guise of 'child protection'. In these institutions, aboriginal children were forbidden to speak their native languages. They were forced to dress as white children and eat food prepared by the institutions rather than living off the land as their ancestors had done for 40,000 years. They had to abandon traditional practices and beliefs, and were force-fed Christian religion. Some of these children, torn from the arms of their mothers, were eventually adopted into white families.

One Aborigine said:

Four generations of my family went without parental love, without mother or father. I myself found it very hard to show any love to my children because I wasn't shown it myself.

The Noongar Tribe of Western Australia

The establishment of relationships between the Noongar people and British Colonists in the Albany area of Western Australia is described in the book *That Deadman Dance* by Aboriginal writer Kim Scott.

Imagine the shock of seeing white men (and the first Europeans in Western Australia were all male) for the first time! When the Noongars recovered from this shock, they are portrayed as wary but respectful insofar as they seemed to view Europeans as equal but very different. Europeans were initially not able to culturally dominate because they relied on the Noongars to locate water and edible bush tucker.

Europeans had a gradual impact on the environment, traditions and lore of the Noongar people. For example kangaroos, a staple in the Noongar diet, were significantly culled after the arrival of white people. The introduction of sheep and cattle fouled water courses and billabongs. There were disputes when Noongars speared sheep for food. Eventually, the indigenous people became dependent on food handouts, including processed flour and sugar which they had difficulty digesting. Alcohol, which had been unknown until the arrival of the Europeans, wreaked havoc.

As time went on, the Europeans gradually asserted their dominance and thought of themselves as superior. Disparaging words like 'nigger' became part of their vocabulary. A white governor was appointed. He and his pronouncements undermined the authority of traditional elders and the lore. The Noongars were banned from entering European settlements unclothed, especially after the arrival of white women. A gaol was built to incarcerate Noongars who did not toe the 'white fella's' line.

The Rabbit-Proof Fence

The film *Rabbit-Proof Fence* is based on Dorothy Pilkington Garimara's book *Follow the Rabbit-Proof Fence*. It relates the real-life experiences of Dorothy's mother.

Set in Western Australia during the 1930s, the film begins in the remote town of Jigalong where three children live with their mother and grandmother, two sisters, Molly Craig 14 and Daisy Kadibil eight, and their cousin Gracie Fields ten. The town lies along the northern part of Australia's rabbit-proof fence, which runs for several thousand kilometres in a north-south direction.

Fifteen hundred kilometres away in Perth, the Protector of Western Australian Aborigines, A O Neville, signs an order to relocate the three girls to his re-education camp. The children are referred to by Neville as 'half-castes', because they have one white and one aboriginal parent. Neville reasons that the aboriginal peoples of Australia are a danger to themselves, and must be bred out of existence. He plans to place the girls into a camp where they, along with all half-castes of their age, will grow up. There is an expectation that such children will become labourers and servants to white families. It is assumed that, if they marry, it will be to lower class white people, thus diluting their aboriginal 'blood' when producing children.

The three girls are forcibly taken from Jigalong to a camp at the Moore River Settlement in the south of Western Australia. However, Molly, Gracie and Daisy decide to escape and walk back home. The film follows the girls as they walk for nine weeks and about 1,500 kilometres along the rabbit-proof fence, all the while being pursued by a white authority figure and an aboriginal tracker. Gracie is recaptured but Molly and Daisy make it home. They head into the desert with their mother and grandmother in a bid to hide.

The epilogue of the film shows recent footage of Molly and Daisy. Molly explains that Gracie has died and that she never returned to Jigalong. Molly also tells how she, as a mother, with two of her own daughters, was once again removed from Jigalong back to Moore River. She escaped with one daughter, Annabelle. A second time, she walked along the rabbit-proof fence, all the way back home.

'We are born, live and die in the cycle of our land'

An indigenous Australian said:

We live in harmony with the seasons of our land. We know when the rains are coming. We know when we can go hunting, and we know which plants are ready to supply food and medicine. There is communion between us and our land. I can talk to God; feel his presence in the beauty of the landscape. I can feel his presence in the freedom of watching the birds, the animals, fish swimming around in the water. We are born, live and die in the cycle of our land.

My Land

An Australian aboriginal prisoner spoke about the importance of his country and how he tried to keep this connection alive through painting while he was in prison:

My dad is from the desert. I'm connected to my father's Dreamtime story, and to his father. Dad told me a lot of stories, gave me the knowledge to paint my father's country. The old people told me stories of the country—that's how I paint. It keeps me connected to my country and the people that live there. I can feel him, when I paint. I keep the country alive through stories and painting. I belong to the land.

Disproportionately Represented in Prison

As harmony with their land is such a critical part of indigenous culture and identity, communities and families
broke down from the time of white settlement. A tragic
consequence of this fragmentation was the particularly high
number of Australian Aborigines who ended up in prison.

In 2012, there were 1,914 Aboriginal and Torres Strait
Islander prisoners per 100,000 adults in their population.
The equivalent rate for non-indigenous prisoners was 129
per 100,000 non-indigenous Australians.

Tragically, the disproportionate representation of indigenous people within the prison system, is accepted as
'normal'. Once again, intergenerational incarceration is
common within this population group.

Apology to Australia's Indigenous Peoples

Kevin Rudd, Prime Minister of Australia, Wednesday 13 February 2008, 9.00 am

I move:
That today we honour the indigenous peoples of this land, the oldest continuing cultures in human history.

We reflect on their past mistreatment.

We reflect in particular on the mistreatment of those who were Stolen Generations — this blemished chapter in our nation's history.

The time has now come for the nation to turn a new page in Australia's history by righting the wrongs of the past and so moving forward with confidence to the future.

We apologise for the laws and policies of successive parliaments and governments that have inflicted profound grief, suffering and loss on these, our fellow Australians.

We apologise especially for the removal of Aboriginal and Torres Strait Islander

For the pain, suffering and hurt of these Stolen Generations, their descendants and for their families left behind, we say sorry.

To the mothers and the fathers, the brothers and the sisters, for the breaking up of families and communities, we say sorry.

And for the indignity and degradation thus inflicted on a proud people and a proud culture, we say sorry.

We, the Parliament of Australia, respectfully request that this apology be received in the spirit in which it is offered, as part of the healing of the nation.

For the future we take heart; resolving that this new page in the history of our great continent can now be written.

We today take this first step by acknowledging the past and laying claim to a future that embraces all Australians.

A future where this Parliament resolves that the injustices of the past must never, never happen again.

A future where we harness the determination of all Australians, indigenous and non-indigenous, to close the gap that lies between us in life expectancy, educational achievement and economic opportunity.

A future where we embrace the possibility of new solutions to enduring problems where old approaches have failed.

A future based on mutual respect, mutual resolve and mutual responsibility.

A future where all Australians, whatever their origins, are truly equal partners, with equal opportunities and with an equal stake in shaping the next chapter in the history of this great country, Australia.

Loss of Identity

Jim is a 'full blood' Indigenous Australian in his 30s. He has been in and out of prison over a number of years because of crimes of violence and burglary. His criminal history has been exacerbated by drug and alcohol abuse.

Jim originally came from the edge of a large provincial town where some of his family are still located. He is still in touch with his Aboriginal heritage and driven by his roots in aboriginal spirituality and culture, in spite of having lived in several urbanised environments at different stages in his life.

Jim works out regularly in the prison gym and exhibits a rather machismo personality and appearance, as many prisoners do, to offset underlying fears of appearing vulnerable.

As an Aborigine, Jim's thought patterns differ from those of 'white fellas'. He is not dependent on linear, logical ways of thinking and reasoning. His thoughts are like stitches in a circular tapestry. Nothing is compartmentalised or isolated; everything is inter-related.

Jim describes our conversations as 'having a yarn'. In 'white fella' terms, it is a laidback relaxed conversation during which we are not clock-watching or working through an agenda. To a white observer, this might appear aimless and disjointed.

When Jim speaks about his life, it appears chaotic. He is of mixed tribal blood. This raises questions about where he belongs and to which group he is answerable in regard to familial relationships, culture and spiritual issues.

Jim's sense of dislocation is exacerbated as he has chosen not to 'go through the lore' and refuses to be initiated into some significant aspects of his indigenous heritage. The very fact that he can now make this choice, confirms the breakdown of culture and community. In common with other aboriginal men, Jim has become complicit in his own loss of identity.

Jim is an accomplished dot painter—a style used originally by aboriginal desert artists to express their aboriginality and spirituality. However, as Jim has refused to be initiated into his tribe, some of his kinsfolk object to him utilising these ancient traditions and images in his art. They say he is not qualified for this sacred work. Jim, along with many other indigenous people, now finds that his spirituality includes elements of European religion, particularly images from Christianity.

Jim has moved around a lot which means, to a large extent, he has lost connection to his ancestral lands. He is asking: 'Who am I?', 'Where do I belong?' and 'Do I have a purpose in life?'

Jim expresses anxiety about his wife and children. He is sick of the chaotic nature of his life of crime and the consequences of being in and out of prison.

He spoke with me about an urgent need to change his thinking and behaviour.

ENJOY

FREE

SMILE!

LIFE

heal-
ing
time.

Feel the fear...

NEED
A
HAND?

Payback

Many prisoners experience desperation when they realise how difficult it is to break free from the cycle of repeat offending. Indeed, many have become so controlled by negative influences that they have no confidence that they can successfully change.

Some prisoners get more and more agitated and anxious as the date of their release approaches. Will they have somewhere to live? How will they be received by their partner, wider family and community? And in indigenous communities there is always the question: Will there be 'payback'?

'Payback' is part of the aboriginal justice system which was operative for millennia before the arrival of colonists. If offences have been committed against aboriginal people, or have taken place in an aboriginal community, 'Aboriginal Lore' may still come into play.

This might include being speared in the leg to cause a significant wound, but not permanent disability or death.

Aboriginal Lore

Aboriginal Lore, or First Nation Justice, is a form of ancient law base on an understanding of life that is very different from 'white fella' perspectives.

While western justice systems are adversarial, Aboriginal Lore is non-confrontational. The accused is expected to be honest and plead guilty if wrong has in fact been committed. In Aboriginal Lore, everyone within the community has a right to speak as part of the justice process but witnesses do not testify in front of the accused as this is perceived to be too confrontational. Indigenous communities accept that is not possible to know 'the whole truth' in any situation. Maintaining eye contact with a person in authority is considered to be disrespectful. The accused is expected to accept the verdict without showing emotion. Indigenous processes seek healing for the offender and to restore peace and harmony to the whole community. There is an expectation that offenders will be reconciled with victims and their families.

Nunga Courts

Indigenous sentencing courts, which include some elements of Aboriginal Lore, began in South Australia in 1999 when a magistrate saw that Aborigines were overly represented in courts and prisons. These Nunga Courts are intended to build trust between the aboriginal and other Australian communities. The magistrate said:

> The consensus among aboriginal people was that they weren't being heard in courts, that it was a club for 'white fellas', which it probably is. [Now] they tell me they trust it and understand.

Some examples of indigenous sentencing courts in Australia include the Koori Courts in Victoria, Murri Courts in Queensland, and the Ngambra Courts in the Australian Capital Territory.

Worth Hearing

Roy is a 'full blood' indigenous man who has been through the lore. He comes from a remote tribal community that has had contact with some of the worst and best effects of 'white fella' society. Alcohol and violence have gradually eroded dignity and traditional ways, as well as the authority of the elders in settling disputes and directing spiritual life. There is now ready access to illegal drugs and alcohol, mindless television and violent video games. On the upside, the community has benefitted from 'white fella's' medical knowledge in diagnosing various ailments and treating them.

Roy has a reputation as a fighter and this deters would-be predators of any sort, even though he is now getting on in years. However, if a prisoner in his unit is vulnerable to abuse, a quiet word to Roy to 'look out for him' is usually enough to keep the bullies away.

Roy is serving a very long sentence for several serious offences. He is an enigma insofar as he is also quietly spoken. He tends not to use expletives and has a faith in God. He attends chapel services, Bible studies and other spiritual activities. Due to shyness he does not say a lot but, when he does speak, what he says is worth hearing.

The Lore Man

Jacko is in his 50s and is highly respected by the indigenous prisoners, and some staff, as an elder, Lore Man and healer. He is a guardian of traditional knowledge that has been handed down through countless generations.

From an indigenous point of view, the Lore Men are informed about the spirit world and have certain powers to manipulate it. They have been given exclusive knowledge and power about traditional places, ceremonies, rituals — where and when they are to take place. Their insights include knowledge of medicinal plants and ways of healing. They are able to divert the effects of spells and curses whose sources may be found in the 'pointing of the bone' or 'being sung' rituals, which can be lethal if the intended victims are conversant with the lore and informed of the action against them.

Jacko was an impressive, quietly-spoken man who kept a low profile. From time to time, he would be approached to help resolve a dispute, give advice, or take action on behalf of a troubled indigenous prisoner.

The Dark Side of Spirituality

Many (but not exclusively) indigenous prisoners have an acute sense of the dark side of spirituality. They understand the source of certain events and experiences as being demonic and turn to the chaplain for comfort and help. In these instances the chaplain needs to be able to respond positively and quickly lest the situation develop into self-harm or worse. Following consultation with the Diocesan Bishop our Ministry response was along the following lines:

Bad Spirit

Lord,
Ernie is spiritually aware,
as the majority of indigenous people are.
It is part of the pattern of their lives.
Ernie tells me that he has a bad spirit in his
    cell.
He is uneasy.
I can see the fear in his eyes.

He wants me to go to his cell and deal with it!
Many of the indigenous guys see chaplains as
    having spiritual power,
Just like the 'feather foot' [shaman] back home.

Oh Lord!
I don't have special power,
– but you do!
Please,
do these things through my presence, voice
    and actions.

The spiritual battle goes on every day.
As usual, I am fearful myself.
In spite of my conviction:
The Spirit of Jesus is the strongest of all the
    spirits!
None can stand against Him!

Lord!
I get this request up to twenty times a year.
I always need to act quickly
– containing fear
– preventing escalation
– avoiding disaster.

I have to be ready to act
(even when I am not ready!)
– spiritually.
You know what I mean!

I will go and do what I can
– with you leading the way!

Later

Lord,
You did it again!
When I got to the wing
and then to the cell
it was a bit creepy.
Other guys crowded round the doorway.
They were quiet
– a bit fearful.

'We are here to get rid of the bad spirit,
that is bothering Ernie.
The Spirit of Jesus,
the strongest of all the spirits
will come!'

[I then read from the Bible]
He [Jesus] went down to Capernaum, a city in Galilee, and was teaching them on the Sabbath.
   They were astounded at his teaching, because he spoke with authority. In the synagogue there
   was a man who had the spirit of an unclean demon, and he cried out with a loud voice, 'Let us
   alone! What have you to do with us, Jesus of Nazareth? Have you come to destroy us? I know
   who you are, the Holy One of God.' But Jesus rebuked him, saying, 'Be silent, and come out of
   him!' When the demon had thrown him down before them, he came out of him without having
   done him any harm. They were all amazed and kept saying to one another, 'What kind of utter-
   ance is this? For with authority and power he commands the unclean spirits, and out they come!'
   (Luke 4:31–36)

Lord
We pray that this bad spirit will now leave,
…that the Spirit of Jesus will come!
The Spirit of Jesus is now here,
bringing change and dispelling fear.
Calm Ernie and the other guys,
Help them to feel better and more relaxed.

Lord,
I pray that this sense of peace and calm will continue.

Robbie's Sick

Lord,
Robbie, one of the indigenous guys is sick.
He's got to a point where he can hardly get out
   of bed.
The medics can't figure out what's wrong.
He is normally a good worker,
and compliant.
So, it's not laziness.

I was asked to talk with Robbie.
When I got to his cell,
he started to tell me about where he was from,
and why he was in prison.

Lord,
He is from a remote community.
His offences have badly affected his mob.
He believes he is going to die.
The 'feather foot' [shaman] 'pointed the bone'
—at him!
Something like sending an evil spell against him.
He believes he can do nothing
but accept this as inevitable death.

Lord,
I told him about Jesus and the resurrection,
that Your Spirit is stronger than
any curse of a 'feather foot'.

Spirit of Jesus, please protect Robbie
Take away the power of this spell
—and also Robbie's fear.
Come, Spirit of Jesus.
Help Robbie to relax,
Keep him close to you.
Watch over him.
Protect him.
Encourage him.

[Three days later]
Lord,
Robbie is back on his feet.
He intends to work tomorrow.
The medics asked me what happened,
   so I told them.
Some of them seem to think:
'It's all mumbo jumbo.'
Others didn't say much.
I pray that in time
all of them will see the truth,
and recognise the conflict
between good and evil.

Grieving for Our Mob

Prisoners rarely get to attend funerals while they are inside. Permission is usually only granted for the funeral of a close blood or similar relative such as a mother, father, husband, wife, partner or child.

Most indigenous Australians do not embrace a nuclear family model. They have grown up in a network of familial relationships, which includes grandparents, aunts, uncles and cousins, which are all as important as direct blood relatives.

Typically, aboriginal prisoners have moved around a lot, so it can be difficult to ascertain who belongs to whom and work out a prisoner's significant relationships.

According to aboriginal culture and custom, all members of a tribe are expected to attend the funerals of certain people. Not to do so is seen as a sign of disrespect and can lead to sanctions under Aboriginal Lore. Memorial gatherings may be arranged in the prison as an alternative ceremony for grieving. These gatherings can be extremely emotional, particularly if the deceased committed suicide or died while in prison.

As the prison chaplain, I had to check out protocols appropriate for such occasions. For example, is it permissible to speak the name of the deceased or display photographs? If the deceased was a member of the Noongar tribe from the south-west of Western Australia then these practices are permissible. However, protocols are different for the Wonggai tribe located 1,000 km north-east of Perth.

As far as possible, it is preferable to have the event in prison on the same day, and at the same time, as the funeral is taking place on the outside. I found it was important to make contact with the bereaved on the outside prior to the gathering, so I could speak about these contacts during the prison service. Sometimes relatives would email copies of the eulogy and order of service so that it could be distributed within the prison.

The most important part of these gatherings was to invite anyone who wished to say a few words about the deceased person to do so. There were always several people who would speak. Another important factor was music and singing. I found a CD recorded by an aboriginal musician to be an invaluable resource.

Attendance at memorials varied between a handful of prisoners to around 80, depending on whether the deceased was well-known and respected within the prison community. Non-aboriginal prisoners were always welcome. It was heartwarming to witness significant friendships being formed as people from differing cultural and religious backgrounds supported each other in grief.

A Yarn around the Campfire

It is a tragedy that so many indigenous people were subject to official policies of genocide, and treated with such contempt. If only the colonists had sat around aboriginal campfires so that they could learn about the ancient rhythms of this country's culture, spirituality, environment and the sacredness of its land. Perhaps then, the outcomes would have been very different.

I value my interaction with the aboriginal people of Australia. Much can be learned from them about spirituality, and the importance of maintaining meaningful, close, extended family relationships. The work of their artists and craftspeople is impressive.

Things are now changing to ways that more appropriately recognise the cultural and personal needs of indigenous people. Sometimes it seems like two steps forward and one step back.

One valid development is legalised discrimination in favour of indigenous people in regard to education and employment. This has enabled some to break through barriers which previously prevented their access to employment, qualifications, promotion and fair wages.

There is still a long way to go — but at least we have made a start.

CHAPTER 7

FINDING GOD IN CAPTIVITY

Doing My Head In

A prisoner got up on to his cell block roof, as a protest. After he had been up there a few hours, the prison authorities sent for a trained negotiator to talk him down. Half an hour later, the prisoner shouted to the guards: 'Where did you get this bloke from? He's doing my head in. Tell him to shove off and I'll come down.'

'Prison chaplains are entirely useless. They are in a class of foolish, indeed, silly men. They are of no help to any prisoner'—Oscar Wilde[1]

Relatively Small Things

In a dramatised production of Wilde's life, the chaplain is escorted around the cells in Reading Gaol to speak to prisoners. The warder unlocks the door and enters the cell, followed by the chaplain. Wilde is instructed to get to his feet and 'stand up straight for the chaplain'. The chaplain inquires if Wilde attended Church of England services regularly before incarceration? Wilde replies in the negative and the chaplain comments: 'If you had, you would never have ended up in prison.' Wilde and his fellow prisoners would have been forced to listen to this individual, Sunday after Sunday.

For more than 200 years, it has been mandatory for prisons in the western world to have a chaplain. This would seem to indicate that chaplains, if they do their work well, can make an important contribution to the spiritual and practical welfare of inmates and staff.

As the prison regime dehumanises people, squashing individual identities and personalities, chaplains have a role to play in enabling people to maintain self-respect, dignity and humanity.

There are simple ways of doing this. For example, almost no-one in prison greets prisoners with a handshake, but chaplains can do this when it is appropriate. On the outside, it is polite to address people by their first name or, in more formal situations, with a title such as Mr, Mrs or Dr. On the inside, prisoners are usually identified by their last name and prison number. Chaplains can ensure that they themselves practise respectful communication. Prisoners are rarely asked for their opinions and, when they are, this is appreciated. Simple courtesies such as 'please' and 'thank you' mean a lot in prison.

While sharing a meal is, in most contexts, a sign of community and good company, prisoners are denied opportunities to interact with family and friends over food. However, chaplains can choose to break down barriers by eating with prisoners.

These relatively small things encourage prisoners to maintain some sense of human connection and begin to think positively. All is not lost. I remember visiting a prisoner in hospital who was badly beaten up. When I arrived at his bedside, he was semi-conscious and, because of the severity of his injuries, could not speak. All I could do was to pray with him, and hold his hand for five minutes. Sometime later, when he had partially recovered, he told another prisoner how much it meant to have the human contact and comfort that he desperately needed at the time.

---

1   H Montgomery Hyde, *The Trials of Oscar Wilde* (London: Dover, 1974).

Eddie's Funeral

Lord,
as you know,
I was asked to take Eddie's funeral.
The undertaker and I managed to thwart the
    media
by changing the venue
at the last minute.

A woman who had known Eddie
…before his offending,
got in touch with me.

She told me a few positive things about him.
Then, she came to the funeral.

Thank you Lord.
That woman enabled me to say something
    positive
…which was true.
I hate funerals that are full of lies
…when the cause of death is never mentioned.

The Grubby Gospel

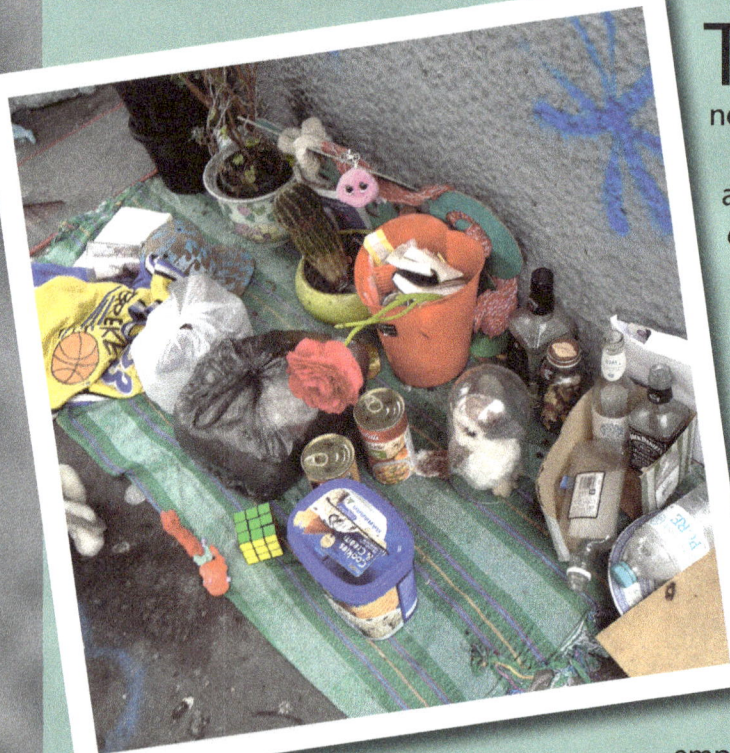

Thankfully, the nature of God, at least from a Christian perspective, has a certain earthiness about it.

God is not to be found only in religious and respectable places; nor is He concerned only with the upright members of society. The circumstances of Jesus' birth in a grubby stable, and his family's escape to Egypt as refugees, immediately identify God with those who suffer, including persecuted minorities, victims of crime and those living in poverty. Jesus, throughout his life, trial and execution, identifies strongly with those against whom criminal sanctions are imposed, including one of the men who was crucified alongside him; 'today you will be with me in Paradise.' (Luke 23:43)

God's involvement in 'grubbiness' is emphasised numerous times in the Bible. Jesus encouraged his followers to provide food and drink to those who were hungry and thirsty, to welcome strangers, provide clothing for the poor, take care of the sick and visit those who are in prison. The word 'visit', used by Jesus, does not only mean 'stopping by and having a chat'. It has connotations of showing practical care for people, and doing whatever is possible to help them in their plight.

In Matthew 25:31–46, Jesus emphasises that whenever anyone visits a prisoner, they are also visiting Him. His hearers were astonished, uttering comments such as:

What do you mean, we visited you? We did not see you in the prison. We visited criminals, but not you?

Jesus insists:

I was there with them, identifying myself with them — all of them.

Jesus is inclusive not only of 'decent' people, but also those who are considered to be morally bankrupt, unstable, cynical, hypocritical, liars, victims of circumstances, those with psychopathic tendencies and those suffering from addiction.

He is saying: 'Look into their faces and you will see me!'

In other words, we can meet God in the most unexpected people and places, through the eyes of faith.

If we are honest, we will see ourselves in people who are in prison. Who among us has not, at some time and in some way, failed morally, been unstable, cynical, hypocritical, told lies, been addicted (to food, television, sex, pornography), suffered from mental health problems and so on? The main difference between 'us' and 'them' is that these traits have not been exposed in us, as they have been in those who are in prison. This is where 'the rubber hits the road' for prison chaplains; as we connect with people in prison, we see both Jesus and ourselves.

Your Brother, the Pope

Pope John XXIII expressed true Christian love to prisoners when he visited a prison in Rome. He went from the grandeur of the Papal Palace to the confines of the prison. He told the prisoners that two of his cousins had been in prison but came to no lasting harm. He said:

> I have come to visit you as your brother. I want my heart to be close to you. I want to see the world through your eyes.[1]

He talked with them as equals — human beings created in the image of God (Genesis 1:27).

Sharing Suffering

'Be mindful of prisoners as if sharing their imprisonment' (Hebrews 13:3)
The majority of people seen by prison chaplains have been ripped out of their usual support structures, leaving them with significant feelings of loneliness and abandonment.

To empathise with prisoners, chaplains need to be in touch with their own experiences of aloneness, abandonment and vulnerability. In this respect, chaplains venture out on a limb, away from the prison as an institution and also from the faith community which accredits and endorses them. They may have a job description on paper but, because of their role and responsibilities, they do not easily fit into clearly defined categories within the prison or church.

Sometimes, churches forget that chaplains spend most of their time in secular institutions, outside churches' usual support systems. Essentially, prison chaplains are, 'shepherding away from home' in what is often a hostile environment, just as the biblical shepherd had to go with his sheep into a hostile environment. As one chaplain has commented:

> So much of our work seems unproductive, is viewed negatively and is an uphill struggle. The loneliness and isolation is quite difficult to cope with.[2]

So, chaplains do in fact share the loneliness, abandonment and vulnerability of prisoners.

The Only Christmas Gift

A group of musicians and singers from the Prison Fellowship Association went into a prison on Christmas Day to sing carols and distribute packs of homemade biscuits and Christmas cards. One prisoner serving a life sentence commented:

> Yours is the only gift and Christmas card I have had for years. I look forward to you lot coming round.

Another prisoner said:

> Why do you come here on Christmas Day bothering about us lot? No-one else does. You should be with your families, shouldn't you?

---

1   William Temple, in the Clarke Hall Fellowship Lecture, 1934, cited in Alan R Druce, 'A Christian Approach to Punishment', *Justice Reflections* 111, 9, at www.justicereflections.org.uk, accessed August 2013.
2   David Scott, 'God's Messengers Behind Bars: An Ethnographic Study of the Role and Perception of the Prison Chaplain in the North East of England', *Justice Reflections* 223, 4, at www.justicereflections.org.uk, accessed August 2013.

Chaplain as Prophet

The pastoral needs in prisons are so overwhelming and intense, that the prophetic side of the chaplain's role is often ignored. However, prison chaplains are called to question the status quo. They need to speak out on behalf of prisoners or staff who are treated unjustly and challenge the tendency for institutions to eradicate individual identities. The chaplain needs to be a voice of encouragement within the prison, facilitating everyone to reach full potential.

The Old Testament prophet Amos was sharply critical of political and religious leaders who neglected the poor. He spoke out, claiming justice on their behalf (Amos 5:24). Chaplains have a similar mandate to speak out on behalf of those who are marginalised and vulnerable within our communities today.

Hope Amid All the Crap

Chaplains, with the help of others, are able to shine a light of hope amid all the 'crap' that goes on in prisons.

Hope in prisons cannot be simply limited to short-term expectations that a judge might hand down a fine or community service order instead of a prison sentence. Most people on remand waiting for their sentence seen by prison chaplains have little chance of avoiding imprisonment, and hope so narrowly defined would be constantly dashed. In other words, hope cannot merely be a conviction that pleasing results will be delivered in the short-term but rather a sense of peace and contentment in the longer-term. Or, as Julian of Norwich put it, in the end 'all things shall be well.'[1] Chaplains can inspire others to believe that, in spite of their failings, they are people whom God loves. Life is worth living. We can play a positive role in society and in the lives of others.

All this is based on a deep down conviction that they have not, and will not, be abandoned by God.

Mother Teresa said:

Let no-one ever come to you
without leaving better and happier.
Be the living expression of God's kindness;
Kindness in your face,
Kindness in your eyes,
Kindness in your smile.

---

1   Dame Julian of Norwich, *Revelations of Divine Love*, Chapter 27.

What Prisoners Say about Chaplains[1]

- If I had a genuine problem — like if my Mum died — I'd like the chaplain to come and check on me, to see if I'm alright until I'm over that period and back to normal. If you've got a problem, the chaplain is an indispensable person, but if you haven't got a problem, the chaplain is classed as a member of staff because they have a set of keys.

- My personality relates to the chaplains. They are approachable; the chaplains listen, unlike the screws.

- It gets us off the wing. The coffee in the chapel is better than on the wing. We have a laugh. The chaplain is good at talking to you, helping you with faith, cheering you up — gives you belief in yourself.

- I keep control of my anger. I came to chapel and it changed my life. The chaplain can pray, or I can pray myself in the cell.

- There is not much a chaplain can do. Although, it is nice to know they are there. You see, the chapel is one part of the prison which doesn't seem like a prison. There are things I can tell the chaplain I can't even tell my Mum and Dad.

- Chaplains are a lot better than prison officers. Prison officers want power and are very macho. There are a few good officers around but they don't trust prisoners. Chaplains treat us like individuals.

- Chaplains are better than staff; some of the staff aren't keen to help anybody. Some staff also tend to go behind the chaplain's back and make things awkward for him.

- At the end of the day, the chaplains work for the prison. So, their first loyalty is to the prison and not the prisoners.

- The chaplain's attitude seems better than the prison staff, but there are some really good prison staff.

- My Gran died recently and they wouldn't let me go to the funeral, so I went to the chapel on the same day. The chaplain's worth it, just because of his help then.

- I don't believe all that religious stuff, but he's okay. He talks to me.

- We sometimes try and get extra phone calls from his office and get him to bring things in for us. But it doesn't work. He's not stupid.

- The chaplain? I'm not into the religious stuff. It's not for me. I'm not sure what he is supposed to do.

---

1 David Scott, 'God's Messengers Behind Bars', 14.

The Spiritual Dimension

Attempts to define the spiritual dimension indicate that there is probably more to human existence than that which is material, logical, psychological and emotional. Put more simply, and relevant to many people in prison, is the idea that as humans we are accepted by a Higher Power. Even while we struggle to understand and name this force of life that is greater than ourselves, we can accept that we are connected and accepted.

Indigenous Australians from the Daly River area of the Northern Territory refer to the spiritual dimension as *Dadirri*. It can be defined as:

> …taking time out for contemplation, listening, being still, finding peace and understanding. This way of being is seen as the Spirit of God working within us bringing a consciousness of Jesus.[2]

The Quakers have similar perceptions, defining the spiritual dimension as an 'encounter' where 'the point is not whether you believe in God, but whether you encounter the Divine, and if so, how?'[3] One of the advantages of the Quakers' perspective is that it does not have dogmas, creeds or leaders. Quakerism puts an emphasis on two things: firstly, the experiential; secondly, 'living out of what they call the four testimonies: peace, equality, simplicity and truth'.

An advantage of taking a Quaker approach to the spiritual dimension of life in the prisons is that you start with a clean slate. There are no pre-conditions. One does not have to do this, that or the other, or believe this, that or the other, to be part of something. Many of the people in prison have never properly engaged with the spiritual dimension of life. The disadvantage of not having this engagement, and not having an encounter with the Divine, is that people are left to their own efforts to cope with life's ups and downs. They have no spiritual help to strengthen, encourage and guide.

---

2 Eileen Farrelly, *Dadirri: The Spring Within* (Darwin: Terry Knight & Associates, 2003), ix.
3 Jill Seggers, 'About Encounter More than Belief' in *Church Times*, 8 April 2011, 24.

The Prison Phoenix Trust

The Prison Phoenix Trust is an organisation that was founded to help prisoners to discover a spiritual dimension in their lives. The Trust takes a holistic approach and encourages the concepts of *Dadirri*, and Encounter, through prayer, meditation, guided exercises, postures and controlled breathing.

Prisoners are encouraged to establish a regular practice, so that, in time, they form a new understanding of the relationship between the material and the spiritual. Through guided exercises, silence and meditation leading to prayer, they experience the love of God who is always reaching out to them.

When people arrive in prison, both their lives and their minds are often in chaos. One prisoner said:

When you're meditating, it's hard to let go and rest your mind because you've clung to things so tightly for so long. At first, everything is turmoil and your grip is so tight. The last thing I wanted to do was to let go. But slowly the fog cleared and I started to move towards the good things around me. I feel I am in the process of spiritual change.[1]

An important part of these exercises is silence, both internal and external. Most of us live our days in a cacophony of background noise. In most cell blocks or wings of prisons, one or more televisions will be on 24/7. We only become aware of the noise when it stops. When it does stop, there is a sense of unease, insecurity, even fear. But guided silence can free us to stop, relax and open ourselves up to the Divine. An ex-prisoner said:

Silence helps you take control of you and find order in the mixed up chaos of everyday life. It introduces you to yourself. It has helped me to find the sun in my heart even on cloudy days and, somehow, I've found a strength and confidence inside, and reassurance that everything will be okay.

---

1 Jill Seggers, 'About Encounter More than Belief', 13.

Another guy describes his daily religious observance:

> When I wake up, and before my mind gets too active, I sit on my cushion, straighten my back and regulate my breathing. After a period of meditation, I ponder on a scriptural text.

It is possible that from this practice, the prisoner then has a significant thought, or a text to focus on for the rest of the day, in spite of everything that is going on around him.

A prisoner with a history of self-harming behaviour said:

> As long as I can remember, I have had this hurt inside. I can't get away from it, and sometimes I cut or burn myself so that the pain will be in a different place and on the outside. After only four weeks of meditating, half an hour in the morning and at night, the pain is not so bad, and for the first time in my life, I can see a tiny spark of something within myself that I can like.

Another prisoner said that mediation was helping him to feel more human:

> All beings, no matter how reactionary, fearful, dangerous, or lost, can open themselves to the sacred within, and become free. I have become free even in prison.

It is notable that practising Muslims rarely come into direct conflict with prison authorities. It seems that their disciplined religious framework of frequent prayer, reading sacred texts, maintaining Muslim dietary law — where possible — and other religious observances enable them to fit relatively easily into the regime. One prisoner explained it as follows:

> My being in prison is the will of God? I don't understand it. I don't like it, but I accept it. There is a purpose that I cannot see.

He went on to say that he had not been abandoned by God, but rather God would console and sustain him throughout his prison term.

On one occasion another Muslim prisoner, who was ill in the prison hospital, asked me to pray for him. I said: 'I usually pray in the name of Jesus.' The response was, 'That's okay. As a Muslim, I have a very high regard for Jesus.'

A Wedding

Lord?
What am I going to do about the request
from Charlie and Pat, to get married in the prison chapel?
He's in here. She's on the outside, at the moment.

Lord,
They are both as mad as a meat axe!
They have these lovey-dovey phone calls,
whispering sweet nothings
to each other for two or three minutes.
The conversation then rapidly
degenerates into a shouting match!
Charlie calls Pat a fucking slut.
She retaliates
…and so it goes on
…until their phone time expires.

When Pat comes to visit,
which she does regularly,
she has so much metal bling on her body
that all the alarms go off!

But Lord,
In spite of all this, they are both likeable people.
They bring a bit of much needed (black) humour into the prison.

Lord!
I usually do everything I can,
to dissuade people from getting married in prison.
But I sense that I need to say 'Yes' to Charlie and Pat.
After all, it may be that they can be happily 'mad' together,
…when one or both of them is not in prison!

When I ask why they want to get married in church,
they are not very articulate,
except to say,
they want Your blessing, Lord.
I am seeing them both tomorrow.
I need your guidance on this one!

Sacred Texts

Most traditions of spirituality and religious belief, though not all, have some guiding principles which are written down in sacred texts. Islam has the Qur'an, Hindus the Bhagavad Gita, and Buddhists the teaching of the Buddha. Jews have the Hebrew Scriptures. Christian Bibles incorporate the Hebrew Scriptures and the New Testament.

Religious workers in prisons are usually free to distribute the sacred texts of the faith which they represent. Christian chaplains are frequently asked for Bibles. One reason for this is that the Bible contains lots of material about 'warts and all' lived experience of human beings. It deals with the harsh realities.

The Psalms in the Old Testament is an ancient collection of passionate songs and prayers for people who are desperate (and that is exactly the experience of many people in prison).

Psalm 88

The angriest, most hopeless is Psalm 88, which illustrates unreserved gloom:

O LORD, God of my salvation,
when, at night, I cry out in your presence,
let my prayer come before you;
incline your ear to my cry.
For my soul is full of troubles,
and my life draws near to Sheol.
I am counted among those who go down to the Pit;
I am like those who have no help,
like those forsaken among the dead,
like the slain that lie in the grave,
like those whom you remember no more,
for they are cut off from your hand.
You have put me in the depths of the Pit,
in the regions dark and deep.
Your wrath lies heavy upon me,
and you overwhelm me with all your waves.
You have caused my companions to shun me;
you have made me a thing of horror to them.
I am shut in so that I cannot escape;
my eye grows dim through sorrow.
Every day I call on you, O LORD;
I spread out my hands to you.
Do you work wonders for the dead?
Do the shades rise up to praise you?
Is your steadfast love declared in the grave,
or your faithfulness in Abaddon?
Are your wonders known in the darkness,
or your saving help in the land of forgetfulness?
But I, O LORD, cry out to you;
in the morning my prayer comes before you.
O LORD, why do you cast me off?
Why do you hide your face from me?
Wretched and close to death from my youth up,
I suffer your terrors; I am desperate.
Your wrath has swept over me;
your dread assaults destroy me.
They surround me like a flood all day long;
from all sides they close in on me.
You have caused friend and neighbour to shun me;
my companions are in darkness.

Psalm 13

Psalm 13 is an example of a prayer of lament. Lament is an often under-utilised resource in western Christianity, but is valuable for providing a connection to a deep existential wail, vocalising it in a way that demands action from God in response to suffering.

How long, O LORD? Will you forget me forever? How long will you hide your face from me?
How long must I bear pain in my soul,
and have sorrow in my heart all day long? How long shall my enemy be exalted over me?
Consider and answer me, O LORD my God!
Give light to my eyes, or I will sleep the sleep of death,
and my enemy will say, 'I have prevailed'; my foes will rejoice because I am shaken.
But I trusted in your steadfast love; my heart shall rejoice in your salvation.
I will sing to the LORD, because he has dealt bountifully with me.

Psalm 46

On the other hand there are psalms that remind us that all is not lost (and God has not abandoned us). Psalm 46 is an example.

God is our refuge and strength, a very present help in trouble.

Therefore we will not fear, though the earth should change, though the mountains shake in the heart of the sea;

Though its waters roar and foam, though the mountains tremble with its tumult.

There is a river whose streams make glad the city of God, the holy habitation of the Most High.

God is in the midst of the city; it shall not be moved; God will help it when the morning dawns.

The nations are in an uproar, the kingdoms totter; he utters his voice, the earth melts.

The LORD of hosts is with us; the God of Jacob is our refuge.

Come, behold the works of the LORD; see what desolations he has brought on the earth.

He makes wars cease to the end of the earth; he breaks the bow, and shatters the spear; he burns the shields with fire.

'Be still, and know that I am God! I am exalted among the nations, I am exalted in the earth.'

The LORD of hosts is with us; the God of Jacob is our refuge.

Psalm 91

Psalm 91 is a favourite of some female prisoners who have experienced high levels of abuse and exploitation prior to coming into gaol because it speaks of the protection offered by a faithful God.

You who live in the shelter of the Most High, who abide in the shadow of the Almighty,
    will say to the LORD, 'My refuge and my fortress; my God, in whom I trust.'
    For he will deliver you from the snare of the fowler and from the deadly pestilence;
    he will cover you with his pinions, and under his wings you will find refuge; his faithfulness is a shield and buckler.
    You will not fear the terror of the night, or the arrow that flies by day,
    or the pestilence that stalks in darkness, or the destruction that wastes at noonday.
    A thousand may fall at your side, ten thousand at your right hand, but it will not come near you.
    You will only look with your eyes and see the punishment of the wicked.
    Because you have made the LORD your refuge, the Most High your dwelling place,
    no evil shall befall you, no scourge come near your tent.
    For he will command his angels concerning you to guard you in all your ways.
    On their hands they will bear you up, so that you will not dash your foot against a stone.
    You will tread on the lion and the adder, the young lion and the serpent you will trample under foot.
    Those who love me, I will deliver; I will protect those who know my name.
    When they call to me, I will answer them; I will be with them in trouble, I will rescue them and honor them.
    With long life I will satisfy them, and show them my salvation.

Psalm 4

Psalm 4, with its images of hope and peace, is often read by prisoners before they sleep.

Answer me when I call, O God of my right! You gave me room when I was in distress. Be gracious to me, and hear my prayer.
    How long, you people, shall my honor suffer shame? How long will you love vain words, and seek after lies?
    But know that the LORD has set apart the faithful for himself; the LORD hears when I call to him.
    When you are disturbed, do not sin; ponder it on your beds, and be silent.
    Offer right sacrifices, and put your trust in the LORD.
    There are many who say, 'O that we might see some good! Let the light of your face shine on us, O LORD!'
    You have put gladness in my heart more than when their grain and wine abound.
    I will both lie down and sleep in peace; for you alone, O LORD, make me lie down in safety.

'Grassed up' Jesus

Prisoners tend to connect strongly with the story of Jesus because he was treated like a criminal. He was 'grassed up' by a mate who was a paid police informer. He was arrested during a police raid, in the middle of the night, and subjected to rough treatment and intimidating interrogation. Jesus was brought before the court, remanded in custody, and abandoned by his friends. He was subjected to police brutality. At his trial, the judge was weak, corrupt and intimidated by the prosecution, into passing the death sentence.[1]

Jesus' story speaks to prisoners about their own personal situations. Here's what a few inmates had to say after hearing about Jesus in a Bible Study:

- Some of that happened to me. The coppers knocked me around.

- The cops kicked down our door in the middle of the night when they didn't need to. I would have come quietly 'cos my missus and kids were in the flat with me. They knew I had a history of violence, so probably thought I would go off at them, but they could have given me a chance.

- At my trial, the prosecutor talked long and loud, a lot more than the defence lawyer. I don't know if the judge was intimidated. He could have been.

- I like the Bible Study group. We can talk about religious stuff that I've not heard about before. I like the sound of this Jesus fella — seems to have been a bit of a tough guy. He didn't let people shove him around.

---

1 Jane Clay, 'Offenders and Their Beliefs', *Justice Reflections* 16, 9, www.justicereflections.org.uk, accessed August 2013.

Eating Pig Food

Another story that Jesus told, The Prodigal Son in Luke 15:11–32, is also popular in prisons. A father has two sons, both of whom would, in time, inherit half of his considerable wealth and land. However, the younger son claims his inheritance earlier than expected. The father immediately gives him his share of the property. The younger son turns his newly acquired assets into cash and sets off overseas, where he spends it on having a riotous good time. He is then in dire straits and desperately needs a job. The only job he can find is minding pigs and he is so hungry that he ends up eating their food. His degradation prompts him to think about home. His father's hired workers would be a lot better off than he is! He realises that he has made a mess of his life and decides to go home, apologise to his father and ask to be taken on as one of the hired workers.

The father has missed his son. He greets him warmly and organises a celebration to welcome him. The other son, who has stayed and worked hard on the property, is so enraged when he realises his brother has returned and that their father is celebrating. He refused to join in the party. The father says to the elder son: '… you are always with me, and all that is mine is yours. But we had to celebrate and rejoice, because this brother of yours was dead and has come to life; he was lost and has been found.' (Luke 15:31–32)

Various prisoners commented:

- The son that went off was a waster. He didn't deserve to be welcomed home.

- Yeah, I wouldn't have welcomed him back.

- It wasn't fair, him coming back like that. No wonder the older brother was pissed-off.

- What about the father who was getting old and had worried about the boy for years? He still loved him in spite of what he had done?

- I suppose it was good for the old bloke. The last time I went back to my family, they didn't want to know — especially after me stealing stuff out of the house to sell and get money for drugs.

- My Dad is a bit like the old bloke in the story. I know Mum and Dad are still concerned about me. Mum will always give me food and takes my washing to do. The old man is a bit more unpredictable but I think he's glad to see me, even though he doesn't say a lot.

In this story and others, Jesus raises the possibility that there may be alternative ways of dealing with human relationships that have gone wrong. In other words, what has happened in the past does not necessarily determine what's going to happen in the future. Ongoing anger, hostility, bad feelings and violence don't have to be the outcome.

Prisoners need to be encouraged to think about responding to situations thoughtfully, rather than always with negative knee-jerk reactions. It is hard to start doing this in prison, but not impossible. The stories that Jesus told have helped people to gradually change.

Prayers and Symbols

Most prisoners view with respect, the place in the prison that is set aside as an area in which religious gatherings take place and religious symbols are to be found. It is the place many will come to for prayer, comfort and conversation in times of crisis. Those who come for prayer might have just received a life sentence with a minimum of 18 years but claim to be innocent. Matters that are brought for prayer include crises within the family on the outside, such as bereavement, an accident, troublesome teenagers, eviction from the family home because of rent arrears, and abandonment by a partner. Prisoners often feel helpless and guilty because they cannot fulfil their family responsibilities.

One group of prisoners developed a 'rule of life', loosely based on the Christian monastic tradition where men voluntarily separated themselves from mainstream society and lived in a monastic community, each having a separate cell. They used Morning and Evening Prayer Services from the *Anglican Prayer Book*. It gave them a framework for their faith which some found therapeutic.

Many prisoners find religious symbols helpful. Ministers of different faith traditions can, with permission of prison authorities, distribute prayer beads, sacred texts and other literature. In the Christian tradition, ministers make available small crosses on chains for prisoners to hang around their neck or keep in their cell. Palm crosses can be stuck onto cell walls, where they can be seen at night if prisoners are uneasy and afraid.

Jewish prisoners may wear a kippah (circle of cloth on their head). Muslims may use the Kufi head cover and Zoroastrians are allowed to wear an undergarment or belt symbolising the armour of God. These and other items give prisoners tangible reminders of another dimension that is not constrained by walls and locked doors.

The gathering together as a group of like-minded believers is an encouragement to faith. Jewish men meet with the rabbi, Muslims meet with an imam. Protestant and Catholic prisoners meet with their respective priests, ministers, pastors (or, ideally, with each other). In the Christian tradition, communion bread and wine are distributed as visible signs of the power and presence of God within the group. One prisoner commented: 'Taking the bread and wine has made me feel clean inside.'

The Most Important Person in the Prison System...

Sam said:

> The prison chaplain and my life have interwoven within the prison system. I first encountered him in the remand prison when I was desperately in need of non-judgemental counselling. That was freely given. Our paths crossed after sentencing when I was incarcerated at a maximum security prison, and again when I was transferred to a pre-release minimum security facility. I came to believe the most important person in the prison system is the chaplain, as he tries to give support, encourage hope, and, through example, Christian love, to people whose self-esteem is almost non-existent. I am certain, without the untiring work of prison chaplains, the prison environment of concrete and despair would be totally hopeless.[1]

Another prisoner said:

> When I came into prison, the chaplain gave me a Bible. I read it, prayed and discovered that it was helpful in my present circumstances. Prison woke me up to the Spirit which pushed me in a different direction. I found I had a choice—between despair, or hope and faith. Choosing hope and faith helped me to calm down and lower my anxiety.

---

1   'Letters from Prison' in *Anglican Messenger* (Perth: December, 1994), 10.

CHAPTER 8

RECONNECTING

Until Things Get Easier

A prisoner typed a letter to himself and doctored an envelope to make it seem as if it had come from his wife on the outside. Most of the content was about domestic problems at home. He showed it to the correspondence supervisor and asked that his partner be allowed extra visits 'until things get a bit easier'. The answer was: 'Yes'.

Loving the Unlovable

Life, without connection with other human beings, becomes dysfunctional and inadequate.

Unfortunately, love is often inadequately perceived as something akin to a 'warm fuzzy feeling'. Many people in prison do not engender such a feeling — quite the opposite. They are not lovable or attractive in appearance or lifestyle. They are 'losers' rather than 'winners'. The ultimate insult in prison is to be called 'a piece of shit'. How do we love someone who bears this label? The best that most people in prison can hope for is anonymity. They usually become high profile for the wrong reasons and when they do they are despised, criticised, vilified, as the lepers of society. The approbation of society is heaped upon them.

To love the unlovable is a genuine act of will. This genuine love is based on a conviction that, at their core, all people are made in the image of God and are valued and loved by their Maker. I once went to a church service in India. As I left, I saw a group of people who were begging. When I got closer, I was horrified by their appearance. They were badly disfigured. Some had ragged stumps where limbs had been and scabs on their faces where their noses had been. I asked an Indian man who they were, and why they looked as they did. He told me they were lepers.

In the first century, leprosy was so feared that lepers were banned from having any contact with others. They carried a bell that had to be rung as they approached others to warn them to get out of the way, so they would not be contaminated. Many people had the perverted belief that their leprosy was a result of their own sin. There is a passage in the New Testament, Mark 1:41 that tells us that a man with leprosy came to Jesus and begged for help (Mark 1:40–45). Onlookers would have been horrified when Jesus, moved with compassion, reached out and touched this man. Elsewhere in the New Testament this kind of approach is referred to as reaching out: with 'a spirit of gentleness' (Galatians 6:1).

People in prison are the lepers of our modern day society. It takes real love to show compassion and reach out a hand of friendship.

'The power of love is not something that is added to an otherwise finished process, but life has love in itself as one of its constitutive elements. Along with water, food, and oxygen.'

— Paul Tillich, *Love, Power and Justice* (London: Oxford University Press, 1954), 26.

A Foul-Mouthed Bully

Tom was particularly unlovable. He was well over six feet tall and grossly overweight. He only showered when threatened by the prison staff, who said that he would be forcibly showered if he did not do so voluntarily. Consequently, most of the time, his presence was offensive, especially in hot weather. He was foul-mouthed (even by prison standards). Whenever he spoke, most of his words came out as expletives. His eating habits were disgusting. His method was to slurp food straight off his plate or to push food into his mouth with his fingers.

Tom was a bully. He would target anyone who was vulnerable in any way, forcing them to hand over tobacco, biscuits and other luxuries bought at the canteen. He indulged in squalid sexual activities and forced these on others. However, he was also a coward and would avoid confrontation with anyone he thought might turn on him to protect themselves or others.

From a human point of view, Tom was just about as unlovable as it was possible to be. Other prisoners and staff had as little to do with him as possible. However, Tom is part of the human race. In the economy of God, there are no exclusions from the commandment to 'Love your neighbour as yourself'. Living and believing in a framework of faith, one must accept that Tom was created in the image of God and is precious to Him.

Incapable of Seeing Anything Sacred or Intelligent

Raimond Gaita picks up Simone Weil's idea that 'love sees what is invisible'. No-one is beyond the reach of God's love, no matter what they have done or how vile they may seem to be. We are all part of a common humanity but our indifference to the suffering of those we regard as outsiders makes them invisible to us. When we dehumanise others in this way, we become incapable of seeing anything in them that is sacred and intelligent — a person that we could love.[1]

In western societies, immigrants are often depersonalised and dehumanised. They are no longer thought of as people, mothers, fathers, grandparents, children, brothers and sisters — but rather only as a block of 'immigrants', threatening to change our way of life. We feel similarly threatened by people in prison.

However, love (which in essence is unconditional and universal rather than tribal) and redemption are always possible. There is, at least, a remnant of a decent core in every human being, even if it is hidden beneath layers of horribleness.

---

1 Raimond Gaita, *A Common Humanity: Thinking About Love and Truth and Justice* (London: Routledge, 2002) cited in Jeffrie Murphy, 'The Case of Dostoevsky's General: Some Ruminations on Forgiving the Unforgivable', *Justice Reflections* 189, at www.justicereflections.org.uk

Bereft of Love

There are people in real life, as well as literature, who seem bereft of love. In Charles Frazier's book, *Cold Mountain*, a man called Inman reflects on his life:

> Worn out as he was, Inman could not rest. A woman had not touched a hand to him with any degree of tenderness in so long that he had come to see himself as another kind of creature altogether from what he had been. It was his lot to bear the penalty of the unredeemed. That tenderness be forevermore denied him and that his life be marked down as a dark mistake.[1]

Another character, Ruby, was supposed to be cared for by her father. When she was seven, he took off for three months to pursue his business of making illicit liquor. Ruby was left to forage in the woods for food, grubbing up roots, sometimes trapping birds and fish. At other times, she was reduced to eating acorns and wild chestnuts. She said that when her father was around, he never hit her.

Then again, he had never patted her head or put his hand to her cheek in a moment of kindness.[2]

Likewise, moments of kindness are a rare commodity in prison.

A prisoner, who has been isolated on death row in the USA for several years, wrote about his loveless existence and some of the things he missed:

> …most of all, to feel the touch of another human being in kindness, to see a friendly smile and hear warm words of love from family and friends. To be sure in the knowledge that you are loved and cared for, to have someone to share the fears and doubts you have, to help chase them away.[3]

1 Charles Frazier, *Cold Mountain* (London: Hodder & Stoughton, 2006), 299.
2 Ibid, 331.
3 *Human Writes Newsletter*, Spring 2013, 18.

'Forgive us our sins...'

From a faith perspective, the love of God is not just an abstract concept. It enables people to bear things and to do things that would be otherwise impossible.

Maureen's husband, Alan, was on his way to church on Christmas Eve to play the organ for the midnight service when he was set upon by two strangers. He was battered around the head so severely that he died a few days later. One of the perpetrators confessed to the murder. The other was tried and found guilty of manslaughter. Speaking about this event, Maureen said how much she had loved Alan, who had been her soulmate for 30 years. When asked about the two assailants, she referred to them by their first names — Ashley and Jonathon. She said she was able to forgive them because of her faith and experience of God's love. In other words, they were not just her husband's killers but human beings made in the image of God.

Maureen is a Christian and her ministry at her local Anglican Church includes being up at the front leading services. She said that, most weeks she, and the congregation, say the Lord's Prayer, which includes a petition that God will 'forgive us our sins as we forgive those who have sinned against us'. Maureen said that if she is to continue in her faith and love of God and ministry at the church, then she needs to put these words into practice. The day after the sentencing of Ashley and Jonathon, she had to give a talk about love at a wedding. It was hard, but she did it.

When Maureen was asked about justice for Alan, and the punishment of Ashley and Jonathon, she said that she expected and hoped they would be given substantial prison sentences — not because she was full of hatred and bitterness or wanted revenge, but because there are consequences to everything we do (for better or for worse). In other words, God's love does not dispense with justice and punishment. What it does do is to forbid punishment arising out of hatred, vindictiveness, revenge, spite, malice and cruelty.[1]

---

1   Interview on BBC Radio 5 Live, 18 July 2013, 10 pm.

Poor Bugger Syndrome

There is love in prison, as in every place where God is to be found, but it does not have a high profile and is not easily found. Oscar Wilde writes of his experience of prison as a loveless institution:

> And never a human voice comes near
> To speak a gentle word:
> And the eye that watches through the door
> Is pitiless and hard:
> And by all forgot we rot and rot,
> With soul and body marred.[1]

The most frequent response in prison, to the sufferings and misfortune of a prisoner, is an impersonal, non-empathic, loveless reaction, which I call: 'poor bugger syndrome'. For example, it was used, on one occasion, by a prison officer to describe a prisoner who had serious injuries after being badly beaten by a group of other prisoners.

> Poor bugger. It shouldn't have happened. He's really suffering, but it's nothing to do with me. I am not getting involved. It's not my problem. It's his own fault. If he hadn't got himself into prison in the first place, it wouldn't have happened.

Many people in prison have little or no experience of love. One offender asked:

> How can I believe in a God who is love, when I have not experienced love in my life? I have been abandoned and grew up not knowing who my parents were.

---

1   Oscar Wilde, *Ballad of Reading Gaol* (first published 1898).

Abused by Christian Brothers

Brian's mother was 16 when he was born. He was taken away from her and placed in an orphanage. He was there until he was six and was then shipped out to Australia as part of the British Child Migration Scheme. Authorities rationalised this by saying the children had no living relatives. In fact, many did have relatives who would have cared for them, given half a chance.

Brian, and several hundred other boys, disembarked in Perth, and were placed in the 'care' of a Roman Catholic semi-monastic organisation called the 'Christian Brothers'. They were mainly lay brothers with a few who had been ordained as priests. They were located about 40 miles from Perth where the Brothers were undertaking a substantial building project to provide accommodation and education for orphans. These boys were used as slave labour by the Brothers. They were compelled to do back-breaking work for long hours, six days a week, and beaten unmercifully if they were considered to be lazy or guilty of some trivial misdemeanour. Other punishments included cold baths or showers in winter, as well as being locked-up in the dark with only bread and water for sustenance. Worst of all, was the sexual abuse that Brian, and many others, were subjected to by paedophile brothers who took full advantage of the boys' vulnerability. Any complaints from the boys were rejected and they were then beaten for telling lies.

Brian survived ten years in this dysfunctional and loveless environment, after which he had to make his own way in life. He moved around a lot and had mainly menial jobs over the years, and eventually ended up in prison, where I met him.

Brian's loveless existence had inhibited his capacity to initiate and sustain long-term relationships. He was a timid man, a loner, who rarely spoke unless spoken to, and, at first, refused to engage in any meaningful conversation. My first encounter with Brian occurred when I found him sitting in an outside area of his cell block. Our conversation was limited to me saying: 'Hi, how are you?'

His one word response was: 'Okay.'

This went on once or twice a week for several weeks, until one day I spotted him in his cell, during a recreation period when the majority of prisoners were out on the oval. I leaned on the door post and said the usual. He invited me in for a cup of tea.

Over several weeks, he started to tell me about his life and, once he started, he didn't want to stop. He had never told his story to anyone before. I didn't do anything except listen, until one day I suggested that he might find it helpful to write down his story. His literacy wasn't great but he could put pen to paper and ended up with numerous A4 pages. With his permission, I referred him to one of the prison psychologists who was a good listener and able to suggest some strategies to help him deal with the past. This worked out well for him. At that time, moves were afoot to get the Catholic Church to take responsibility for the abuse that had occurred in their establishments. Brian's transcript was, with his permission, eventually rewritten and became part of the evidence presented to a public enquiry.

All Brian needed was a patient listener and some gentle prompting to enable him to unburden himself. His horrendous experience with the Brothers had made him resistant to any kind of organised expression of religion and it didn't feel right to press him. He allowed me to pray for him once or twice, and I told him God loved him, in spite of his experiences at the hands of the so-called 'Christian' Brothers, who were not representative of the Christian faith. I went away on leave and, when I returned, he had been unexpectedly released. I never saw him again. I think of him from time to time and hope that, having found someone who was prepared to listen to his story, he was able to move on with his life.

The Only Difference Between Us

Jimmy was a real hard man who people didn't mess with, if they wanted to stay whole and healthy. He was also hostile towards anything to do with spirituality, religious ritual, chapel services, chaplains, imams and religion … full-stop. Hostility exuded from him; his body language and attitude indicated contempt.

He demonstrated this one day when he walked into the chapel courtyard, where a lunch had been set out for a group who were meeting in the chapel, and started to eat. I had to go outside and point out to him that the chapel courtyard was out of bounds, except for those who were at the meeting. I also had to ask him to stop eating and leave. When he ignored me and carried on eating, I went round to his side of the table, stood next to him and asked him again. He turned and eyeballed me from about twenty centimetres and asked me what I was going to do about it (if he continued to ignore me). I said that I didn't want to have to call security but, if he didn't do as I asked, I would have no choice. (In all the years I worked in the prisons, I had only ever done this once before, during an occasion when I thought there was going to be a ruckus between three prisoners, with one of them facing the prospect of getting seriously hurt.) Jimmy continued to eyeball me for about ten seconds and then grabbed a sausage roll and left. Later, I reflected on the possibility that he could have turned violent and done me serious injury, but I never thought he would. Subsequently when I saw him around the prison, he continued to be silently hostile.

Most, if not all, other staff members confronted with the same situation would have, quite rightly, called security. This would have been without really considering the consequences for Jimmy, which could have been serious. A few would have relished the opportunity to 'put the boot in'. I did not want to inflict trouble on him when it was not necessary and because of a relatively minor incident. If I had been in his shoes and spotted some food which was rather better than I would normally get, I may well have done the same. The only difference between him and me was that he was a prisoner and I was not.

Walt Whitman compares himself to prisoners in his poem 'You Felons on Trial in Courts'. Speaking of himself he writes:

> Beneath this face that appears so impassive
> Hell's tides continually run …
> I Feel I am of them — I belong to those convicts … myself.
> And henceforth I will not deny them — for how can I deny myself.[1]

When Christmas came round that year, as usual I accompanied a group of musicians and singers going around the cell blocks singing carols and distributing cards and gifts. I didn't know which block Jimmy was in until I came across him by chance, among a lot of other men. As I handed a card and gift over I said: 'Merry Christmas' (as we did to all the guys).

He smiled at me and said: 'Thanks.' From then on he was never friendly, but neither was he hostile to me.

From a faith perspective, Jimmy and I are both the same in the sight of God. W H Auden summed up the reality when he wrote: 'Love your crooked neighbour with your crooked heart.'[2]

---

1   Walt Whitman, *Leaves of Grass* (New York: Vintage Books, 1992), cited by Jeffrie Murphy in *Justice Reflections* 189, 16.
2   W H Auden, from 'As I Walked Out One Evening' in *Collected Poems* (New York: Vintage Books, 1991), cited by Jeffrie Murphy in *Justice Reflections* 189, 15.

Love and Animals

People, who have difficulty in the giving and receiving of love in human relationships, may be able to make a breakthrough assisted by interaction with animals. While serving a prison sentence for manslaughter in 1916, Robert Stroud murdered a prison guard. He received a death sentence, later commuted to life imprisonment with no hope of parole. Due to his propensity for violence, he was moved to Leavenworth Prison in Kansas where he was placed in solitary confinement. One day in the exercise yard, he picked up an injured bird, took it back to his cell and looked after it. The prison authorities decided to allow him to start breeding canaries and do research on them. The hope was that, in putting his mind to something positive, he would be easier to handle.

That turned out to be the case.

I observed over a number of years, how some people who do not seem to be able to nurture loving relationships with other human beings, could do so with animals. Another 'lifer' had an affectionate relationship with a cat. It used to come to his ground floor cell window in the early evening, on most days. The man would let the cat in and feed it, after which it sat on his lap purring as it was stroked. Knowing this guy's background, his loving relationship with the cat seemed incongruous.

At another prison, staff initiated a fish-breeding programme. Supervised prisoners cleaned out the tanks and set them up for incoming stock. One prisoner commented:

> I like it in here. I find the combination of water and fish, comforting and relaxing. The fish seem comfortable, relaxed and not in a hurry. I hope to be like them one day.

Something I Had Never Felt Before

I had got to know Sammy over several years when he had been in and out of gaol. I noticed on the admissions list that he was back again. Sammy came down to see me and we shared a pot of coffee together. He told me that last night he was sitting in his cell thinking about his past, present and future. He told me his story (some of which I already knew). He was 30 years of age. His involvement in criminal activities began when he was a juvenile. He and a mate assaulted an elderly woman and stole her handbag for drug money. They thought they had got away with it and so decided to do it again, but they were caught the second time. He was only 14 but robbery with violence is a serious offence and he ended up serving eight months in juvenile detention.

When Sammy was released, he teamed up with some kids he had got to know inside and became involved in a variety of criminal activities, mainly connected with buying, using and selling illegal drugs on the streets. He and others were caught again and this time he was sentenced to a ten month stretch in the same detention centre.

Again he was released and was determined to dissociate himself from his former 'friends' and life. He struggled to find decent accommodation and had a series of menial jobs over a few months before he succumbed to an invitation to get back into the drug trade.

Over the next ten years, Sammy was in and out of prison several times. Over that time, he had a number of relationships with various women also in the drug trade and fathered a child. During those years, his health had gradually gone downhill due to increased drug use, his lifestyle and anxiety about the threats made against him by drug dealers.

He and a mate, whose life had followed a similar pattern, decided to do an armed robbery to pay off debts, then move away and make a fresh start somewhere where they were unknown. They armed themselves with replica hand guns (neither their victims nor the police knew they were replicas) and attempted to rob a liquor store late one evening.

Their attempted armed robbery was a disaster. There were more staff on duty at the liquor store than anticipated, one of whom ran out of the shop and phoned the police on his mobile. The men panicked, fled empty-handed and were picked up by armed police several streets away. They were very fortunate the police did not shoot them, as they had been reported as armed.

At the time of our conversation, Sammy had just received a seven year sentence for armed robbery. His past, present and future looked bleak. If he survived his sentence (and it was a big 'if', because of his debts to drug dealers, some of whom were in the same prison), what would his future be? As far as he could see, he had no future and no hope of anything better.

He said, for the first time ever, he had had thoughts about 'topping himself'.

I was reminded of a book I once read, *Despair: A Moment or a Way of Life?* [1] It seemed to me that Sammy was on the cusp of despair becoming 'a way of life' for him.

I said to Sammy that neither he nor I, nor anyone else, could change his present

---

1   C Stephen Evans, *Despair: A Moment or a Way of Life?* (Illinois: Inter-Varsity Press, 1971).

circumstances. The first thing he had to do was to accept them, and take responsibility for being where he was, rather than making excuses or trying to blame someone else (as he had done in the past). Second, I said I had some Good News for him. He perked up at this. Probably because good news was something that Sammy had not had for a very long time. The Good News was that God loved him, and so did I, along with a number of others, in God's name. I asked him to read aloud a passage from the Bible which describes part of the Roman execution procedure to which Jesus and two criminals were subjected. We talked about the attitude of these two criminals to Jesus. One rubbished him. As far as we know, Jesus did not respond to him. But the other admitted his guilt and appealed to Jesus for help and, because God loved him like He loves us, the criminal got the help he needed (Luke 23:39–43).

I said to Sammy that I knew that in the past he had read the Bible and prayed, because we had previously spoken about it. I went on to say:

I am going to give you a Good News Bible and a list of passages to read, one for each day. In regard to praying, start by turning the television off, sit in your chair for ten minutes and pray by saying, 'Lord God, please make yourself known to me.' And sooner or later, He will. If you want to, we can talk a couple of times a week for a few weeks. And, if you are willing to take responsibility for yourself and do what you need to do, things will start to change inside you. Also, think about attending our weekly chapel service on a regular basis and enrolling in one of our Sycamore Tree programmes where you will be able to hear from prisoners about how life is changing for them, as well as hearing about the experiences of victims.

I then outlined some practical things that would help him, and some that would not. I suggested that he put his name down for a job, enrol in a course in education, use recreation time to get physically fit and be compliant with the prison regime. My advice was to not get involved in the drug scene in the prison in any way whatsoever, because it would be bad for him physically and mentally and further complicate his debt crisis.

I told him that God was always reaching out to us in love and it's up to us to respond positively. After that, I read the following words from a prisoner about experiencing God's love:

I ended up doing this Christian programme. It's a programme designed to help people and I thought, oh well, I'll give it a go. I felt something I had never felt before, which was love. I never had it in my life when I was younger—and I couldn't stop smiling. I smiled for three days. My jaw was sore. It was unreal.[1]

When I left the prison two years later, Sammy was making slow, but steady, progress. There had been some setbacks, which were to be expected but, overall, there was change for the better and the beginnings of a sense of hope for the future. Sammy chose to accept God's love into his life.

---

1   Neer Korn, *Life Behind Bars*, 192.

CHAPTER 9

LIFE BEYOND PRISON

The Most Important Thing

A man in prison for a motoring offence said: 'The most important thing I learned in prison was that I could use my artificial leg as a device in which to smuggle all sorts of things into the country.' He is now a successful smuggler in London, living in a big house in a posh suburb.

Fear of Freedom

In the film *The Shawshank Redemption*,[1] a prisoner who has been incarcerated for many years, comments about the surrounding walls topped with razor wire:

When you first come here you hate them. When you have been here a long time you get used to them. Then you get to a point where you can't do without them.

He is referring to people who cannot cope with life on the outside after serving long prison sentences. The film shows two prisoners, both incarcerated for more than 20 years, being released at different times and placed in a hostel. Both hang themselves shortly after.

---

1   Film *The Shawshank Redemption* (Directed by Frank Darabont, 1994).

Home?[1]

I walk outside the prison gate
People are looking at me, they know I'm a crim

Throw away the key

Most people won't forgive
Why should they trust me?

Throw away the key

I feel awkward, out of place
How can I start again?

Throw away the key

Give me a chance,
Don't keep punishing me!

Throw away the key

I'm a real person
I've got feelings

Throw away the key

How can I start again?
I don't belong out here

Throw away the key

Home is prison
More home than out here

Throw away the key

---

1   I was inspired to write this poem in response to ideas
    shared with me by Reverend Emeritus Professor William R
    G Loader.

Getting Out and Staying Out

Key factors influencing whether a person will manage to stay out of prison after their first experience of incarceration include:

- education and basic literacy skills;
- employment to provide income and create a sense of purpose;
- mental health management and regular use of medication when needed;
- maintenance of physical health, regular meals and access to medical treatment;
- support and treatment for drug and alcohol addiction;
- life skills such as cooking, cleaning and financial management to counter-balance the effects of institutionalisation;
- financial planning and debt reduction strategies;
- supportive family relationships and other social networks;
- availability of suitable accommodation.

Prisoners often lack supportive relationships as their history of offending, and often drug and alcohol abuse, have had a negative impact on family and friends. Without supportive, caring and loving relationships, individuals are emotionally cast adrift with no point of reference. Such lack of support places prisoners at particular risk if they have no options but to return to their old crime connections when they are released. This is especially true if offenders have had high media profiles.

When prisoners have no option but to return to areas where they committed crimes, this poses difficulty for their own support, as well as that of their victims. In such circumstances, former prisoners need to be circumspect about the places where they are seen in public, especially for the first year or two. No doubt, word will quickly get round that they are 'out'. One former prisoner tells how he avoided going down a particular street because he knew his former crime associates were still drug dealing from one of the houses. If they spotted him, he would be invited in and could very easily slip back into his former criminal lifestyle.

Getting out of prison sounds easy, but those who have been in and out tell a different story. The following accounts highlight experiences of prisoners and ex-prisoners who have been 'in' and 'out'.

I Love Prison

Jenny said I was born in prison. My mum was in here when she had me. I've been in institutions most of my life. My mum couldn't look after us kids, so we were taken away — children's homes and stuff. Some of them were okay. It depended on the staff. Others weren't though. Some cruel buggers ran them. My trouble is, I get angry a lot. If someone says something I don't like, I mouth off at them, sometimes lash out. I do it in here as well and then I'm sorry. I've given the staff shit. They know me though, and they're okay. I do love prison. I'm safe here and it's like coming home. I'm 22. I know I've got to change if I want to live long. I'm not sure about that. Last time I was out, they put me in a flat, a tower block in a rough area — tenth floor. It was like being in a sweet shop for me — cheap booze and drugs. You could get anything you wanted.

I Feel Safe Here

On two occasions, Suzie has been involuntarily detained in a mental health facility for her own safety, and the safety of the general public, after ingesting a mixture of drugs and alcohol. She has also overdosed on more than one occasion and has had to be hospitalised.

I've been in prison here lots of times. Prison's got a routine, a structure. I feel safe here. I've got friends. When I'm close to getting out, I get anxious. I cry and don't eat. It's scary out there. I haven't got family. Well I have, but they don't want to know. I've pissed them off so many times — I can't go to them.

I've Got a Room and a Bed

Another prisoner said:

Last time I was out for five months. I was starving out there — buying drugs. I hardly bought any food. I ended up living in a stairwell. It was winter and cold. I'd do anything to get money for my next hit. I was begging in the streets. I didn't care if I lived or died. I didn't have a shower for weeks. I was filthy. In here, I've got a room and a bed, and meals. I'm on the methadone programme. I know I can't go on as I was. I am 29 now. I have to get a grip and do something different. Coming back here is the easy option for me.

Booze, Drugs and Sex

Simon was going to be released, for the eleventh time, and this time was going to try to go straight. His most recent sentence had been his longest — six years — and he knew any future sentences would be even longer. He was 38 and had been in and out of prison since he was 14, and was sick of it. When released in the past, all he had been interested in was getting back into the booze, drugs and sex. He knew that's what his mates — inside and outside — would expect. In fact, he hardly knew anyone who wasn't doing drugs and crime.

Up until this point, he had knocked back probation, serving full prison terms so that, when he got out, no-one would be looking over his shoulder. This time he would be on probation and his release was conditional on him living in nominated housing and following other rules. As his release approached, he became more and more anxious, waking up in the early hours and chain-smoking. Was he doing the right thing? In the past he had been quite violent. However, this side of him had started to diminish as he got older, partly because younger, fitter guys were coming through the ranks and he knew he would cop beatings if he treated them aggressively.

On his release he was met at the gate by two people. One was from the probation service and the other was the manager of the hostel in which he had agreed to live. He settled in and was briefed about how the place ran and reminded of the conditions of his parole — to keep off drugs and booze and not to associate with ex-offenders, including his former mates. He said:

It felt very strange to be back on the outside. I was bit paranoid. A few days later, I was sitting in a cafe in Parramatta and felt everybody was looking at me. I got wound up and nearly said to one bloke: 'What the fuck are you looking at, mate?' I was up for a fight but he walked out and I realised he wasn't really looking at me. It was me looking at him. Later, I was talking to a bloke at the hostel who had been out a few weeks. He said the same had happened to him and we had a bit of a laugh about it.

I had to go to the social security office for an interview and fill in a million forms to get the dole. The bloke who interviewed me was okay. He knew my background and helped me with the forms. Soon I've got to start applying for jobs. I don't know how that will go. Who wants to employ an ex-con who hasn't worked for years? A couple of days later, I decided to catch the train down to Bondi. I spent a lot of time at Bondi in the past. That's where some of the 'action' was. I was a bit anxious about running into my old mates and getting involved again. But unless they've changed, they will be in bed till midday and not out and about till the middle of the afternoon, so I should be right.

Eight months later Simon was back in gaol for relatively minor offences. He hopes he will not have to serve out his whole parole period and says he is still determined to live differently:

With my history, I didn't do badly. Next time, I'll aim to be out for a year — if I manage that long, it might go on from there.

No-one Gives a Shit

Rosco had been in and out of prison several times, mainly because of low-level drug dealing. He bought drugs on the streets and sold them, taking a cut for himself. In his late-20s, he didn't want a future locked into the uncertainties of the criminal underworld. So, he persevered with his intention to stay out of gaol but it was difficult. He said it would have been easier to survive if he had returned to crime.

While he was in prison, he obtained a qualification in industrial cleaning but found it hard to get a job on the outside. He applied for 23 jobs but only managed to get two interviews. The majority of prospective employers did not even acknowledge his application. At both interviews, he was asked: 'Where have you done the job before and for how long?' His chances were not helped when he admitted that he received his qualification in prison and had never actually worked in a full-time job.

Things became complicated for Rosco when he missed an appointment to see his probation officer because of an administrative error. A letter informing him of the date, time, and place, did not arrive until the day after his scheduled appointment. Due to his failure to attend the appointment, his social security benefits were cancelled and he was left without money for four weeks. He lost 12kg in weight. After his benefits were reinstated, the authorities accused him of not trying hard enough to get a job and he was once again penalised.

Rosco said:

How am I supposed to live? I went without food for a few days. On some days I was able to borrow a few dollars and get some pot noodles or a bag of chips. I am being threatened with eviction from my hostel because they were not able to take my $50 rent out on the weeks when my benefits were cancelled. I can't pay them back until things change. I feel depressed and suicidal. I am trying as hard as I can to keep all the rules so I can keep out of gaol but no-one gives a shit. At the hostel, people are always getting their benefits stopped. Sometimes it's their fault but not always. Administrative 'fuck-ups' occur too often. I get the message that some bureaucrats think all ex-offenders are scum and they would be glad to see us all back in prison. I don't want to go back to prison, but it's tempting when I am hanging around with no food and I could easily go out and make plenty of money doing a few deals.

Support Services and Survival Tips for Life Beyond Prison

A strong theme that came out of researching this chapter was that there are now a lot of community development projects which are operating at local levels, loosely connected to global networks. There is a grassroots 'push-back' against institutionalisation and bureaucracy. People are deciding at local neighbourhood level how to feed the poor among them, but the people who most need this help are at risk of missing out on accessing it, if more is not done to publicise the 'under the radar' projects which are now forming.

Interestingly, a lot of research bodies are now emphasising that we should not be talking about 'resettlement' or 'reintegration' into communities after prison experiences, because most prisoners do not have good community connections prior to incarceration. So, while they tend to be 'under the radar' community projects are great from a local responsibility point of view. The downside is that people who lack community networks or have poor communication skills, might not be aware of what is now available within their own housing estates and suburbs.

Project coordinators of soup kitchens and other community development projects where meals, bread and other resources are freely distributed, commonly affirm the fact that many low-income and homeless people, including people recently released from prison, are increasingly accessing these community-based 'under the radar' projects, they often operate at night when clients do not have to talk to anyone else or be seen. Some community gardens and 'food swap' stalls are now installing safety lights so such people can access free food during the night while maintaining dignity.

The following organisations operate in many countries and have websites with local information:

◆ Prison and Court Chaplains

A great network of chaplains from a wide variety of faith traditions works in courts and prisons throughout the UK and most other countries. Contact the relevant prison or court administration for referral details.

◆ Prison Fellowship

Prison Fellowship is a Christian ministry operating in many countries in the world which aims to bring hope to prisoners, ex-prisoners, their families and others affected by crime by working to make communities safer. Prison Fellowship volunteers visit prisoners in adult, youth and immigration detention facilities. The Prison Fellowship is motivated in its support to prisoners' families by evidence that criminality can be intergenerational in families affected by incarceration. It says:

> Today's children of inmates are in danger of becoming tomorrow's inmates unless we give them hope for the future.

The fellowship programmes include Angel Tree which enlists the cooperation of local churches to provide Christmas gifts for prisoners and their families.

Other programmes include: Art from the Inside; children's camps; mentoring; social enterprise programmes, such as Second Chance; and restorative justice initiatives, such as the Sycamore Tree Project.

The Fellowship provides a range of voluntary work opportunities for former prisoners. These include marketing and administration, prisoner and family support and project participation.

◆ Practical and Spiritual Assistance

It would be true to say that those who claim to have a religious faith are morally and ethically bound to offer practical as well as spiritual help to some of the most needy people in any society, for example those being released from prison. Almost all the mainline churches and representatives of other religions are involved in chaplaincy work in the prisons in most

Western Countries. They also offer a variety of comprehensive aftercare, over and above the statutory obligations for assistance, for those being released from prison and their dependants. Localised religious or charitable communities often run food banks and provide basic necessities like white goods, furniture, crockery and cutlery, bedding, curtains, etc. to enable an individual and/or a family to make a new start. This often includes personal friendship and support. Having people around who are trustworthy and supportive makes a huge difference as they seek to regain their place in mainstream society.

◆ Prison Network Ministries

Prison Network Ministries provides holistic support to women who are (or have been) in the prison system.

The network's work is inspired by the Bible verse: 'Remember those who are in prison, as though you were in prison with them.' (Hebrews 13:3)

Programmes include: art/craft; sport/fitness; Fun with Mum days; Christian discussion groups; mentoring; court support; children's camps; and a post-release support programme called Side by Side.

Voluntary work opportunities include: prison and post-release support for other families; transporting children of prisoners for family and social events; staffing children's camps; administration; marketing and fundraising.

◆ Kairos Prison Ministry

Kairos is an international independent Christian ministry which reaches out to people who have experienced imprisonment, their families, friends and those who work with them. It runs four programmes:

- Kairos Inside;
- Kairos Outside for Women;
- Kairos Outside for Men;
- Kairos Juvenile.

These are delivered as short courses and weekend events which create space for people to reflect on their lives and future choices. Kairos Outside for Women provides opportunities for families to participate in weekend retreats with time to share with others who have been through similar experiences. Former prisoners are encouraged to strengthen their relationships and support structures while also reviewing their attitudes and behaviour. This opens the way for positive change.

Kairos Outside for Men provides opportunities for men who have been in prison and their male supporters to spend time together reflecting on the impact of their experiences.

Kairos short courses and retreats are followed up with ongoing personal and small group support as well as bi-monthly reunions.

◆ Alpha Caring for Ex-Offenders

Alpha operates in many countries around the world. Prisoners wishing to connect with their local church after they are released can seek referral to Alpha's Caring for Ex-Offenders programme. A support worker from the programme will visit them in prison to assess needs and risks. Alpha then negotiates with a local church congregation to ascertain whether they have the capacity to support a prisoner with integration into their community.

Alpha provides training to the church community and then a mentor from the congregation begins visiting the person in prison. When the person is released, the mentor meets them at the gate, assists with initial appointments and basic transitional needs. Other church members are encouraged to provide support by helping the person to write résumés, fill in forms and prepare for job interviews. This increases friendship and social support networks.

Alpha continues to provide ongoing support and training to the church.

◆ Anglicare

Anglicare is part of the worldwide concern of the Anglican Church to provide support and practical help to those in need. Consult country and community directories for services offered.

As an advocate for disadvantaged people, Anglicare's work is grounded in the values of care, dignity, respect, hope and change. Its latest research emphasises that everyone needs and deserves an affordable and safe home.

◆ The Salvation Army

The Salvation Army is a worldwide organisation renowned for its care of, and assistance to, those in need. It provides an extensive network of court and prison chaplaincy services including Christmas gift distribution to prisoners and their families. Other services include: housing and crisis support; alcohol and drug rehabilitation programmes; counselling for gambling and other addictions; family tracing; domestic violence advocacy and support; soup kitchens; emergency financial relief; and other community support.

◆ Colleges, Universities and Public Libraries

Some prison support services have agreements with colleges and universities which provide continuity with training options and post-release work placements. Colleges and universities also provide support with: housing; employment options; résumé writing; health; literacy; chaplaincy; and other student services. There is a range of clubs on campus which provide social, educational and recreational opportunities.

◆ Neighbourhood Houses and Local Churches

Neighbourhood houses and local churches provide many free food options which can help to stretch the budgets of people who are newly released from prison. Frequenting such locations can be a way to pick up tips and also information about courses in cooking, budgeting on a low income, literacy and job search skills.

Many estates with government-funded housing have Community Information offices which provide referral to support services within their local neighbourhood.

Increasingly, neighbourhood houses and churches offer free community meals, providing 'free stuff' swap tables and distributing fresh fruit, vegetables and bread in cooperation with various agencies.

ABOUT THE AUTHOR

Paul Gill has worked as an Anglican Minister in Australia and England. He has spent most of his ministry working in places where the majority of the population live in challenging economic and social circumstances. This included ten years working as a prison chaplain in maximum security prisons. These years of prison ministry were the most satisfying of his working life. 'I always felt I was engaging with people about things that really mattered.' He and his wife, Anne, currently live In Hereford, UK

If any reader(s) would like to make contact with the author they can do so via the publishers, Waterside Press.

PAUL GILL
578361

Confessions of a Prison Chaplain

Mary Brown Foreword by Juliet Lyon

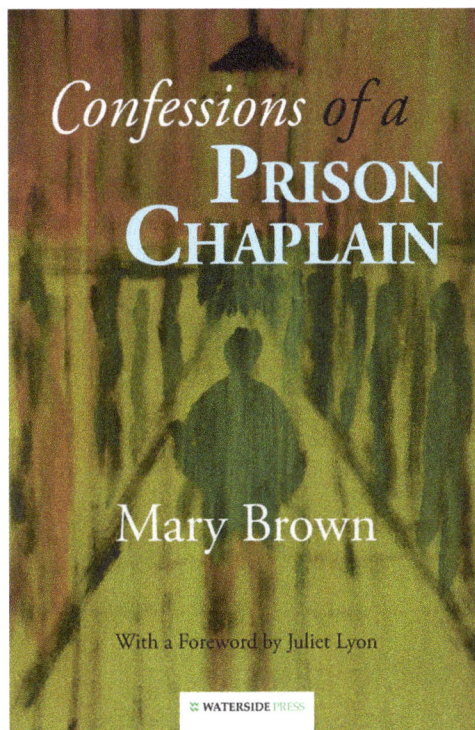

Mary Brown's engaging book describes the lifeline work of prison chaplaincy. It shows how important to prisoners this contact is and how it blends into the ever-pressing world of prison regimes. Among topics covered are the duties of chaplains, forgiveness, 'prison chapel goers', Christmas in prison, bad news, grief, anxiety, learning in prison and restorative justice (as old as religion itself). Contains insights for people of all faiths (or none) and reaffirms the importance of pastoral support in the reform and rehabilitation of prisoners.

'A valuable read for those currently active
in or contemplating prison ministry'
friendsjournal.org

'Engaging, thought-provoking … contributes to our understanding of the hidden, often neglected world of prison'
Juliet Lyon (From the Foreword)

Paperback & ebook | ISBN 978-1-909976-04-7 | 2014 | 136 pages | Waterside Press

www.WatersidePress.co.uk